INTRODUCING ECONOMIC ACTUALISM

············ SECOND EDITION

Making the Science of Rational Behavior More Rational

DAVID BILLINGS

authorHOUSE®

AuthorHouse™
1663 Liberty Drive
Bloomington, IN 47403
www.authorhouse.com
Phone: 1 (800) 839-8640

© 2016 David Billings. All rights reserved.

No part of this book may be reproduced, stored in a retrieval system, or transmitted by any means without the written permission of the author.

Published by AuthorHouse   01/19/2016

ISBN: 978-1-5049-7335-9 (sc)
ISBN: 978-1-5049-7333-5 (hc)
ISBN: 978-1-5049-7334-2 (e)

Library of Congress Control Number: 2016900565

Print information available on the last page.

Any people depicted in stock imagery provided by Thinkstock are models, and such images are being used for illustrative purposes only.
Certain stock imagery © Thinkstock.

This book is printed on acid-free paper.

Because of the dynamic nature of the Internet, any web addresses or links contained in this book may have changed since publication and may no longer be valid. The views expressed in this work are solely those of the author and do not necessarily reflect the views of the publisher, and the publisher hereby disclaims any responsibility for them.

KJV

Scripture quotations marked KJV are from the Holy Bible, King James Version (Authorized Version). First published in 1611. Quoted from the KJV Classic Reference Bible, Copyright © 1983 by The Zondervan Corporation.

To my parents, who always supported an awkwardly actualist son in his struggle with a strangely nominalist world

Contents

Preface ix

Chapter 1 Overview 1
Chapter 2 Certain Deviation 43
Chapter 3 Uncertainty 99
Chapter 4 Social Confusion 131
Chapter 5 Econo-Addiction 171

A Tale Of Two Viewpoints: Nominalism And Actualism 191
Afterword 195
Index 197
About the Author 201

Preface

Mention the word "economics" and three quarters of the room will roll their eyes. Economics has often become the subject that confines and torments us, rather than the subject which unites us and frees us. This book aims to unite through its understanding and to liberate through its truth. Yet in the process it may strike some nerves by examining some assumptions that underpin our society. In fact, it examines the process of assuming itself.

Economics is meant to be the study of rational behaviour. Rationality should be liberating, leading to a happy life that affords for fun in its place. Yet this is not economics' reputation. It has often been called the "dismal science". I hope to make economics less dismal.

Economic actualism holds that society is essentially a "confusion of nominal and actual wealth". The failure of traditional economics to deal with this confusion in a systematic method is what makes it dismal in the eyes of so many. The work "economy" stems from the Greek words for "house manage", but we have abandoned this sensible goal for the dismal goal of nominal wealth in the form of national economies, corporate growth, international trade and stock prices.

But economics is just one, though a central one, of the humanities. As economic actualism works to unravel the confusion of nominal and the actual, it overlaps into other areas of study. So while economics may seem a dismal science, by improving its shortcomings we will hopefully make all

David Billings

of our lives a little better and our let our spirits burn a little brighter. This is an exploratory book about uncharted territory in the middle of our existence. I hope the discovery process eases your burden.

David Billings,
B.A. (Commerce/Economics), B.Sc. (Eng.)

Chapter One

Overview

Our economic theories don't work anymore. Perhaps, they never did. Capitalism, socialism and communism all seem outdated. The political leaders who sell them so slavishly seem out of touch with economic realities. Our society, and even our planet, can not afford these dogmatically held errors for much longer.

If capitalism says mankind's history is that of "dominance over nature" and communism says man's history is "class conflict" and socialism promises "redistribution through centralized systems" then economic actualism has a new thesis; that mankind's history is "the confusion of actual and nominal wealth".

The process of measurement is problematic in any science. Yet it is a problem which has suffered great neglect by the science of economics. Economic actualism has been boiled down the study of how nominal and actual economic reality differ into three main branches of study: the uncertainty which is created by the act of economic measurement, the manners by which nominal and actual economic data are certain to diverge, and the social feedback systems which help to keep the first two principles under control. At the present time in North American society, our neglect of all three of these principles are combining to mechanically subvert the quality of our society.

Economic Actualism is a new view on economics, and society. This is the first published account of the theory. Interestingly enough, you do not have to abandon capitalism, Marxism, socialism, Keynesian economics or any of the other mainstream ideologies in order to agree with economic actualism.

Economic actualism does not belong to either the political left or right. It sees value in both. However, it is believed that economic actualism brings other economic ideologies into a different light.

Economic actualism gives this new perspective by differentiating between nominal and actual economic data.

Economic actualism strives to discover the means by which the nominal recording of an economic statistic can differ from the actual reality. Without a method to find the single actual economic datum, behind the nominal, we are faced with a seemingly endless number of possible realities when we make a decision. We need a method to find the actual situation behind the nominal façade. Our leaders decide on the macroeconomic scale. But everyone also makes decisions on the microeconomic scale. Economic actualism provides this method.

The factors which increase nominal wealth while decreasing actual wealth, or decrease nominal wealth while increasing actual wealth, can be uncontrollable if left unchecked and are a grave danger to us both as individuals and as a society.

By applying economic actualism, we keep our participation in the economy closer to what we actually intend.

One of the beauties of economic actualism is that it can be summarized in three short principles. The first two are truisms.

The third is that the first two create confusion. This simplicity makes it easy to comprehend. Yet it should also make it easy to expand into areas of social complexity without losing focus.

Introducing Economic Actualism

Economics affects each of us on the personal level, where simplicity is valued. Yet it also effects our society in all its complexity, where the ability to deal with this complexity is essential without losing important aspects of the situation. Many previous theories seem to miss mentioning these three principles.

Economic actualism then, has three essential principles:

1. UNCERTAINTY

In addition to the problems of economic measurement due to diversity and quantification, economics is set by the problems of the uncertainty principle: the act of measuring rational behaviour can alter the definition of rationality.

2. CERTAIN DEVIATION

Some social phenomenon are certain to occur which deviate nominal economic records from actual economic reality. An inversion occurs when a decrease in actual wealth is an increase in nominal wealth, or vice versa. Inversions come in two manners: externalities and ineffectiveness. Economic inversions due to externalities include: spirituality, leisure, preventing damage, environmental issues and idolatries. Actuality can also differ from nominalism due to loss of effectiveness such as financial obligations, conflict, dependence on centralization and error. Inefficiency can be seen as a source of error. Inversions are a subset of deviations, as deviations look at the total quality of life.

3. CONFUSION

The confusion of actual economic status with nominal economic status is a common source of social conflict and debate. Social mechanisms are required to constantly keep the damages from the first two principles in check. Implicit in the economic actualism is the idea of "econo-addiction".

Econo-addiction is defined as an unhealthy obsession with nominal economic wealth to the neglect of actual economic wealth. Econo-addiction can be both macroeconomic and microeconomic. It can affect both the individual and the community.

Our society has become obsessed with the idea that our nominal economy must grow every year, even after our actual economy such as our environment, freedom from bad debt, and lifestyle is threatened. Yet despite these actual losses we continue with hazardous nominal economic growth because without this growth, we will not get paid. That may sound crazy, but it is sadly often the truth.

The world is going crazy and economics, the study of rational behaviour, is leading the descent into madness. This descent can be described as the result of not differentiating between the nominal and the actual. The study of economics has well described the "invisible hand" which allows free markets to self-regulate. The action of consumer demand and producer supply, which can be illustrated by supply and demand curves, brings markets into an equilibrium of price and quantity. But as we shall discuss, the "invisible hand" is often that of a pyromaniac sparking a match.

Price and quantity are the nominal values which traditional economics limits itself to. Price and quantity are the lifeblood of economics, but they are not the lifeblood of a life.

Value and worthiness are the essence of life but these pose a problem for traditional economics: they are not measured. Price and quantity data are readily available. We all want value and worthiness, but economics delivers only price and quantity.

When we search for value or worthiness using systems that provide only price and quantity and provide no method to estimate the difference, we can get overwhelmed by the infinite number of possible realities the nominal figures depict.

These possible realities gain a life of their own, while the actual economic reality becomes an anonymous face in the crowd.

As a result, many of us sadly give up on creating actual wealth. Nominal wealth seems easier to create. We have certifiable numbers from nominal wealth that tell us what progress we are making. The numbers are a quantifiable measure which we come to analyze, even if the instrument which calculates these figures is malfunctioning. It is simpler to accumulate as many nominal figures as possible, then convert them into the actual value and worthiness we planned for in the early stages of life. Yet it is easy to get addicted to the nominal and lose sight of the actual completely.

Econo-addiction is the obsession with creating nominal wealth, even at the expense of actual wealth, an exercise in speciousness. The problem of a price's inability to describe value is as old as society itself. Yet the history of the twentieth century is predominated with frustration with the discrepancy between nominal and actual wealth. Ideologies such as fascism and communism arose from the frustrations and disappointments from economies that promised much and delivered less.

This obsession with nominal growth increasingly threatens our society. Nominal growth is encouraged, even when it undermines actual growth because we view actual growth as an almost mythological creature we can not account for. If we can not account for it, how can we pursue it? Many of us have given up on trying to find value and worthiness. We have settled for price and quantity.

©Alphaspirit – Dreamstime.

Figure 1 Econo-addiction is the obsession with increasing nominal records of economic wealth even when it results in a decrease in actual wealth.

Econo-addiction is as real a threat to our society as drug addiction. Both are popular because they create feelings of euphoria amidst a reality of stagnation. Like drug addiction, econo-addiction is a source of delusion which makes us happy in the short term but miserable in the long term. A large proportion of our people and our institutions rely on nominal economic status for their pay before an eventual conversion into some form of actual wealth. But it is easy to lose sight of the actual, and become obsessed with the nominal. The nominal has numerical figures attached to it which render an illusion of irrefutability. The nominal can have rules which provide structure while the actual can place responsibility on the individual he may not feel prepared for. It is easy to covet nominal wealth because it can be so easily seen and "verifiable". It comes largely from society while actual wealth, ultimately, comes from within. Nominal wealth, such as money, may not be the goal itself. But for the love of money, many will subject themselves to many sorrows, actual poverty. The love of money, nominal wealth, is the root of all evil. (1 Timothy 6:10).

Our addiction to nominal wealth at the expense of actual wealth takes many forms. But it's good to consider how other forms of econo-addiction work when considering a specific form of econo-addiction. None of us is totally free of nominalism. We all are at heart, actualists living in a nominalist society. While it is the actual wealth we want, we are in the habit of acquiring it as a result of nominalism. We can not just instantly rid ourselves of our nominalist society. Even if we could, we are creatures which, due to our biology, have a strong dependence upon society and so will always, in this life, be partly dependent upon nominalism as a stepping stone to actual wealth. The problem must be managed. We shall have an overview of the entire process of how we diverge from actualism into nominalism before looking more specifically at each aspect. We must choose actual economic growth if we are to create a sustainable society.

THE FIRST PRINCIPLE: UNCERTAINTY

The Uncertainty Principle applies to economic measurement, meaning the measurement of rational behaviour can alter our definition of rationality. By measuring our economic activity with money we can alter our perception of rationality and suffer great losses, perhaps even our society, our freedoms, our joy or our planet.

Economics, which deals with the production and distribution of resources, attempts to analyze how rational people should behave. It studies rational behaviour using methodical analyses of supply and demand. But the free market mechanisms of the "invisible hand" require that economic participants have freedom of choice, that they are free to make choices of their own design. This also requires that they participate in the economy of their own free choice. Yet many times, at least almost all of the time in the "modern" economy, the choice to participate in an economy is largely due to duress. Much of our ability to protest our economic participation is silenced.

Consent comes in three varieties: fair agreement, duress and consent from silence. Consent from fair agreement is where both parties to an agreement know all of the variables in an economic exchange, see no foul play in them and freely agree. Consent from duress is where one or both parties verbally agree in order to meet some dire need such as a mortgage payment but feel pressured or uniformed. Consent from silence happens where at least one or both of the parties is involved without verbal consent due to ignorance of parts or the whole of the agreement, or just being quiet about objections.

A perfect currency would be one where cash value equals real value, one that is fair. However, a perfect currency with value has never existed and may never exist. Even in heaven, where everyone has wealth beyond measure, people will be fair but currency may not be needed there. And in Hell, where people are in bonds of misery, currency may not be in use either. Perhaps purgatory could provide a perfect currency and allow men to purge the bad economic habits they developed in this life. But in this life, any currency in use is imperfect. While other books in this series use the word currency to describe other communicative symbols, in this economics book "currency" refers to "money".

"Silence is consent" is a cliché but we all follow it. As a hypothetical situation you are in a small garment shop and spy seven candies in a bowl by the register. You are bored and hungry so you call out asking if it is OK to have a candy. No one answers so after a minute of waiting you eat a candy. The shop keeper then comes out, furious. She has 7 young children, a set of young quadruplets and a set of triplets. Her customers are so cheap she could not afford Christmas presents so all the kids think they are "bad". She wants to take them out for a special walk in the park but you have ruined it since now seven kids will have to fight bitterly and tearfully over six candies. But you protest your innocence. "I didn't know".

While this may seem silly and extreme this is a common situation in economic transactions. We just don't know about some injustices in our economy. The victims are silent so we assume consent. Gold is an example. Gold is gold and whether it is mined by involuntary slave labour from ancient Mexico or a modern union mine, it all goes into a yellow bar. Its history is usually silent.

©Nicolae Gherasim – Dreamstime.com

Figure 2 While the Bible says little about purgatory, it has captured the hopes of many as a possible means for them to repent of this life's sins without facing eternal damnation.

The good mixes silently with the bad. We can not tell the difference and gold has played a substantial part in the economy, even if we don't own it. The modern global economy may be similar. An auto may have steel mined in union shops or in Chinese slave labour camps, but we don't know which.

We may think that slave labour is irrational, but our purchases may have silent consent to their practice. If money is a communicator, we communicate through some purchases that such irrational practices may exist but that we don't care about them enough to prohibit them. By measuring with the currency of a present business cycle, we unknowingly but silently alter the perception of reality.

The assumptions of the business cycle are in every economic transaction, particularly in a complex modern economy. We engage in a transaction with the assumption that the laws and customs of the moment are followed. Due to either duress or silent ignorance we do not have the time or ability to verify element in production. The International Standards Organization, ISO, has made attempts in this area, but it is cumbersome and imperfect and often a threat to proprietary methods.

Every culture or every business cycle has customs which make the process more liquid yet which require silent consent but which might result in dissent if made known. These assumptions change over time. The business cycle can result in our definitions of rationality being changed by the economic transaction. Often we come under increasing duress or silence due to the momentum of a business cycle. Philosopher Henry David Thoreau wrote how most men lead "lives of quiet desperation". They are separated from the simple life they desire by a business cycle that seems out of balance and out of touch with men's' real needs. Yet through lack of time, resources or verbal skill, they remain silent in their desperation. The second principle of economic actualism also affects this process.

Many major changes are happening to currencies in recent decades which are being met by dangerous silence. Take the USA for example, though Canada is roughly similar. In the sixties we had fiat or paper money which was backed by gold reserves. United States paper money had to have gold backing it up. With US military and cultural victories, this currency system became globally popular and the United States dollar became the currency of international trade. The underlying culture of this gold backed currency celebrated a combination of social and natural resources.

However, with very little discussion President Nixon took the United States off the gold standard, some say because the gold in Fort Knox was stolen. The United States then had a strictly fiat currency that had no backing of physical resources but this currency seemed to reflect the cultural celebration of America's social strength. Such a change should ideally have been a major political issue to generate fair agreement. But the criticism was relatively silent compared to the magnitude of the issue, perhaps due to the government's perception that it was in duress.

This fiat currency economy was short lived however. Somewhere in the 80's or 90's we switched from a fiat type currency to a credit type economy. The majority of transactions were not based on gold free fiat money, but with obligations to pay fiat based money. Credit cards were invented decades ago, but they basically took over by the nineties. Again such a major change to the economy should have garnered criticism but a combination of perceived duress and silence allowed it to occur. This was the second major currency change.

However, the economy is changing again. While debts have risen and become the major form of transaction, derivatives or credit default swaps are rising to now take their place. Again, the discussion is slight compared to the magnitude of the phenomenon. The total derivatives market is estimated to be approximately one quadrillion US dollars worldwide. If we were to divide this one quadrillion dollar market between the one billion people in the developed world, the figure would come to one million dollars a head. A family of four would have 4 million dollars from derivatives if divided on a per capita basis.

It does not matter if you know what a derivative is, it is still a currency. Some bushmen in the jungles of the Amazon do not know what a credit card is, yet they are a major form of currency you probably take for granted. The derivatives market now dwarfs the credit card market yet it has generated very little discussion or regulation. There is a chance that many pension funds, banks,

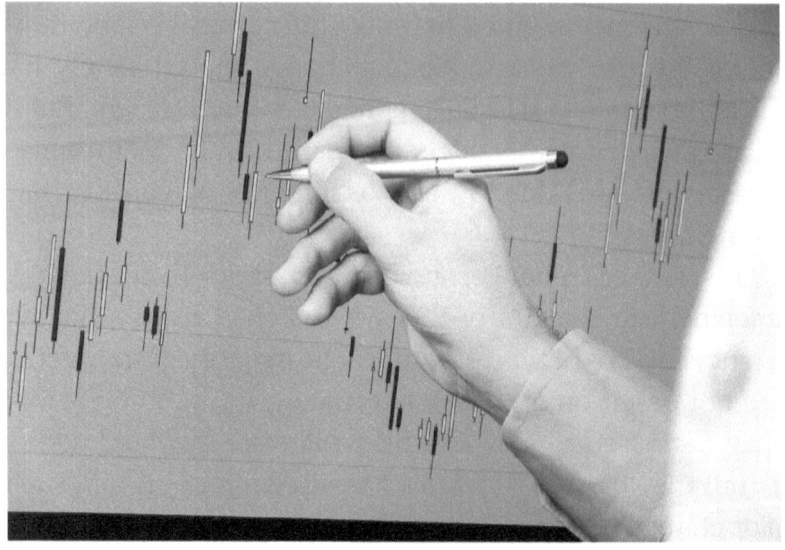

©CreativeImpression – Dreamstime.com

Figure 3 Derivatives are complicated formulas used for insurance purposes which have exploded recently with very little regulation.

Introducing Economic Actualism

© Allesio Moiola – Dreamstime.com

Figure 4 Some people still remain in the world who are not accessible by credit cards such as those in the upper regions of the Amazon basin. We might see them as nominally poor, though they may think that we are actually crazy.

corporations or governments will suffer from these currencies due to trades they don't understand. They may also show up in mortgage values we don't understand.

Yet all of these currencies: the gold backed fiat, the fiat, the credit currency and the derivatives style currency, have come in with little discussion. Many people in America were comfortable when the fiat currency came in and may not have felt duress. But with perhaps due to the Vietnam War no one in the government seemed to mount a strenuous opposition.

It can be said that these currencies have come in largely without the awareness of the vast majority of the public at the time. The consent has been silent. Yet there is a certain momentum to any currency. While a derivative may be a pointless and perhaps bogus computer formula, a credit card is a worthless piece of plastic and a dollar bill a worthless paper, the decision of so many to use them in the measurement of rationality has given them value. Aside from barter, every currency has this uncertainty.

There is an actual value of an economic product, say a widget, which is hard to quantify. But this value exists before the currency is applied. The use of currency to measure this value alters the definition of rationality, giving it a new, nominal value which also exists. If this widget must be purchased as part of an economy of uncontrolled debt it can lose actual value while the nominal price increases.

The currency, like a derivative, may gain value by associating itself With widgets. This value also exists. But part of both surviving in a modern economy and influencing a society in a positive manner requires us to at least try to determine these two values: the value of the widget before measurement with a currency and the value of the widget after measurement with a currency.

An economy where people, lands, goods and services have more value before economic measurement than they do after economic measurement becomes unstable. A healthy economy is one where the value after economic participation is more than the value before or outside of economic participation. Man is a social being and naturally participates in an economy. But he also has an individualistic nature which, unlike many animals, is constantly consciously evaluating the society and the economy he participates in.

If it seems to you that the retort to silent consent is to speak up, you would be correct. However, so many issues can exist in a modern economy and some externalities and ineffectiveness can create duress. Media is often overwhelmed with issues and also concentrated in few corporate hands. And credit run media is our major communications method in the credit run economy. Likewise, many political leaders in the credit based economy are also selected on the basis of their ability to raise credit. For example, running for the US presidency can now run close to a billion dollars in cost for a job that pays less than one million dollars per year. The currency is a means of communication as well as measurement and so questioning the prominent currency of the day can be difficult.

The other problem is that for everyone on the outside who tries to speak, there is someone on the inside who seems to be increasing his skills at not hearing them. This lack of hearing can seem like deliberate self-delusion, but to those with a huge inventory of some currency with imbued value behind it, such as derivatives, maintenance of such a currency can seem like a valid priority.

The use of a currency is a central social and economic issue, but many issues exist. They all compete for consideration. The sublimation and repression of these issues into the subconscious is a major psychological and sociological force. But this sublimation gives nobility to modern society which I plan to discuss in "The Politics of Economic Actualism". Sublimation and repression are stressful but exploited by modern salesmanship.

Economic growth often increases the number and intensity of issues increasing the weight of sublimation on our psyches but in the search for more nominal economic growth, we have a tendency to increase the number of issues both on others and ourselves. For many of us, the actual wealth we seek may be a simple as a couple of hours of peace a day. But under the pressures for nominal growth, we lose this actual wealth. Our ability to deal with the issues we have hidden in our subconscious may be lost as well. Yet we continue to seek the nominal in a descent into econo-addiction. Deviation, the processes which confuse nominal records and actual, add fuel and oxygen to the spark of duress.

David Billings

THE SECOND PRINCIPLE OF ECONOMIC ACTUALISM: DEVIATION

The first principle of economic actualism states that the act of measuring rational behaviour with imperfect currency changes the value in uncertain ways due to consent from silence and other factors. The second principle "deviation", says that some behaviour can increase nominal wealth while decreasing actual wealth, or vice versa, in ways that are quite predictable, yet, almost certain to occur. Like Death and Taxes, economic deviation is inescapable. All that we can hope to do is postpone and mitigate the effects. Deviation of actual economic status from nominal economic status comes in three main classes: externalities, idolatries and ineffectiveness.

EXTERNALITIES

Externalities are effects produced by rational behaviour which are not measured by the currency. Unlike problems like silent consent of the first principle, externalities are predictable. But they require analysis by sciences outside of economics. However, despite our recognition of these losses, they still occur.

These externalities can not only create damages which are not measured economically creating actual loss, but they can also be a source of nominal wealth, inverting the relationship between the actual reality and the nominal measurement. Perhaps the largest sources of externality are environmental issues, spirituality, leisure, prevention of damage and error.

Environmental Issues

Environmental issues are perhaps what are commonly brought to mind when externalities are considered. In the early twenty first century, environmental damage is becoming both an increasing threat to our actual wealth and a dominant force behind the growth of our nominal wealth. While it is our actual wealth that we actually desire, unfortunately we can tend to make decisions based on our nominal wealth status. Once we make such a decision we can find ourselves trapped in what seems to be a certain, even inescapable, descent into nominal wealth at the expense of actual wealth.

We have all heard of many issues: global warming, deforestation, drought, invasive species, extinction etc. But I will briefly consider one example for descriptive purposes: overfishing. It is quite possible to catch fish with your bare hands, at least it was in recent history. When I was eight on vacation with my family in Northern Ontario I once caught a brook trout by tickling its belly and throwing the sleepy fish onto shore. Historically, many people caught fish this way but with very little nominal records. Catching fish with bare hands is immensely satisfying, a great source of actual wealth, but no nominal wealth. As fish became rarer and rarer, we progressed from hands to spears to hooks and nets. Each progressive step resulted in more nominal wealth, in the form of fishing equipment, to catch the same fish or actual wealth. This, and an infinity of other examples has led to the confusion of our society.

Eventually, overfishing occurs and we must then add travel costs to get to new types of fish which may be less palatable. Boats are then required. Boats use expensive gasoline, more nominal wealth. But this gasoline and the associated oil leaks poison water bodies and, again, decrease actual wealth in the form of fish stocks while increasing nominal wealth. As recently as the 1970's, experts were claiming that the oceans were an inexhaustible source of food which could feed the human populace for the foreseeable future. This seemed necessary since arable farmland was becoming scarce. But already fishing boats are travelling to remote waters of the globe like some Ahab in search of dwindling fish stocks. Whereas, once boats had to go to remote places for the profitable whale, now it is to replace the once ubiquitous cod.

The point of economic actualism is not that environmental damage is bad. This point has been made by other schools of economics. Economic actualism seeks to emphasize that while overfishing decreases actual wealth, it increases nominal economic growth. Sailing to remote seas in diesel fuelled fishing liners is big business that shows up on traditional ledgers as assets.

Our nominal growth is encouraged, while our actual growth diminishes. It seems like an inescapable spiral into the trap of nominal wealth. Many environmental issues may be analyzed this way.

Spirituality

The erosion of spirituality also erodes actual wealth while increasing nominal wealth, a theme common in literature. If spirituality is the ability to find happiness regardless of your worldly circumstances, then it is the ultimate source of actual wealth. Yet in a society obsessed with demand side economics, which seeks to increase economic wealth by increasing economic demand, spirituality can be seen as a threat to our nominal wealth.

The modern age has become obsessed with creating demands for instant gratification to a multitude of needs, a common theme of modern commercial art. Our need for nominal economic growth is often adversarial to our need for actual spiritual growth. Yet we seem at times to be inescapably sliding into the pit of commercialism.

Leisure

Related to spirituality is the actual wealth of leisure. While leisure is often confused with spirituality, the two are recognizably different. In fact, some cultures find spiritual wealth in the process of work, such as the Amish with their fine furniture. Yet leisure is a different activity.

Leisure, meaning our time off of registered employment, is a fundamental human need and effective leisure is essential for a society and an economy. Leisure allows us to consider modifications to the business cycle. It allows us to create and explore, the basis of our future economy both nominal and actual.

Leisure allows us to rest and to dream, renewing our minds and bodies for the tasks ahead. Leisure is also a means of stimulating nominal economic demand while increasing actual economic wealth. People spend money when they are not working. Entertainment, fitness, home improvement and education are examples of things that people need spare time to purchase. In doing so, they improve societal actual wealth and economic wealth simultaneously, so long as their spare time is effective and not dragged down into unspiritual matters.

Yet much of modern economics seems to treat leisure time as an enemy. Full time employment is the objective, even better when it involves long commuting times in costly cars and decaying roads. In many ways, leisure is

©Nyul – Dreamstime.com

Figure 5 Leisure can be utilized well in any manner of ways, many of which will lead to economic growth which is both nominal and actual.

dangerous to nominal economic growth only because it offers people alternatives to the present business cycle. Every business cycle relies upon a set of commonly held assumptions and laws. While leisure allows men to question the validity of such assumptions, it also gives men an opportunity to validate these assumptions. An economy which views leisure as an adversary may be an economy that feels it has something to hide, and is unstable.

Prevention of Damage

While a stitch in time, may save nine, the nine can be recorded as a source of nominal wealth

©Juliengrondin – Dreamstime.com

Figure 6 Our habits of commuting create nominal wealth as we buy gasoline, cars and road construction but they create actual poverty of lost time, poor health and environmental damage.

Introducing Economic Actualism

©Philcold – Dreamstime.com

Figure 7 Some engineers believe that the paint on the Hindenberg dirigible was flammable and caught fire from a static electricity induced spark during refuelling in New Jersey after a transatlantic flight. That small fire spread on the skin and ignited the hydrogen gas inside the balloon.

while the one, which can have much actual wealth, escapes detection. Prevention of damage is a source of actual wealth that often escapes nominal measurement. But in our obsession with nominal wealth, we have created a disposable society with decreased actual wealth.

Error

One man's error can be another man's wealth. If a road needs to be rebuilt due to shoddy original workmanship, the result can be an increase in nominal wealth with a decrease in actual wealth.

Inefficiency

Inefficiency, the process of doing the right thing poorly, is traditionally seen as contrary to ineffectiveness. However, inefficiency can be seen as a source of error. For example, a bureaucracy that uses paper inefficiently can be a source of profit for a paper company as it has not made paper conservation one of its priorities.

IDOLATRIES

Idolatries are just a different word for brands. Branding is an essential business tool and an equally essential component of society. In a complicated world, brands help both the consumer and producer focus on what a product, institution, religion, belief, or public figure stand for. Having a sign on the door that says "Cancer Society" helps workers to remember to keep their political beliefs and home carpentry projects outside. The "Cancer Society" sign on the door also tells people who visit what to expect.

Idolatry, the creation of false value in a predictable direction, is a ubiquitous problem. Each word we use is a brand and much of both eastern and western philosophy is concerned with the problems of how words reflect reality. But in economic transactions, producers actively compete for brands, to be an idol of the economy. Producers compete so that they will have the "coolest" clothing line, the tastiest candy and an infinite number of other brands. Yet institutions have brands as well.

Religions compete to be the "one true path to God", or at least the best way to him. Schools try to project images of excellence in their field of study. Governments try to show that their society, and currency, is the best. Neighbourhoods and municipalities can develop unwarranted reputations. The problem of idolatry, the use of words that create an unwarranted reputation for either good or bad, seems universal.

The problem of idolatry differs from the uncertainty in the first principle. The first principle deals with uncertainty that arises from the process of measurement. Idolatry is the inescapable process of creating untruths during social interaction, the scam that is predictable in any sale but which still occurs. An idol uses words to create value while an icon conveys meaning. Externality is damage to a product or quality of life which can invert the relationship between actual reality and the nominal measurement.

Idolatry is talk that is damaging to understanding while the first principle describes a situation that can confuse us and compel us to suffer in silence. The first principle of uncertainty compels us to participate in an entire economy whose products we realize are mispriced but which we sell and consume anyway under duress. Idolatry can lead to ineffective behaviour, but idolatry is different. It is a process of communication and misunderstanding caused by aggressive salesmanship which can lead to ineffective behaviour, whereas the use of icons should increase understanding and improve behaviour.

INEFFECTIVENESS

Ineffectiveness is doing the wrong thing well. We can set out to accomplish a goal, excel and accomplish our task and then discover it was a fool's errand. Ineffectiveness is a set of forces which restrict or limit our ability to make the right choice such as financial obligations, conflict or dependence on centralization.

When we lose our ability to choose outside of an inversion and are compelled to participate due to duress, an economic bubble results. This can occur in our own life or an entire society.

Financial Obligations

Indebted behaviour is recorded behaviour, and as a result, nominal behaviour. We can do many acts outside of a debt relationship: charity work, work for the family, barter transactions, art work, etc., but they may not be recorded and thus are not nominal wealth. Yet when people become trapped in financial obligations that record almost every minute of their life as an economic benefit, they become obligated. When new opportunities arise, or when demands lessen, those financial obligations become a source of ineffectiveness. We do something very well, but it becomes the wrong thing to do. Financial obligations can commit us to ineffective behaviour, decreasing actual wealth, while they overstate our nominal wealth.

In the early twenty first century, many people, in fact many countries, are constricted by debt. Both lender and debtor have become bound by the obligations they have previously entered. This can create liquidity problems and a host of economic ills such as unemployment, unmet economic needs and products without demand. Yet the debts are encouraged partially because they increase nominal wealth.

Conflict

Conflict is good for the nominal economy but can be deadly for the actual economy. In fact, conflict may be defined as nominal growth which is created by the loss of actual wealth of another, or the potential to create that loss. Consider war. Military spending can become immensely expensive, yet it is a source of employment and shows up as economic growth. Yet war can become the ultimate destroyer of actual wealth. The world's modern economy has produced weapons of immense power, claiming to be wealth. Yet as a result, we all live under the threat of total global annihilation.

Conflict can be classified as an inversion if the set of your analysis includes both the winner and loser of the conflict. And many economic processes have elements of inversion, ineffectiveness and duress. However, conflict is a source of ineffectiveness regardless of the set used for analysis. Peacemaking is difficult and once a conflict is set in motion, it has a strong tendency to restrict choice.

Dependence on Centralization

Dependence upon centralized institutions is a source of nominal wealth, but often it is to the detriment of economic methods that can be more effective. This takes numerous forms. But a prominent example in today's society is the decline of the family in favour of centralized institutions such as schools or old age homes. The family is a source of actual wealth that escapes nominal measurement.

Yet man is by his essence a social animal. Centralized power, if only in a small tribal unit, is an inevitable need of man. Mankind could gladly rid itself of all error, environmental damage and other forms of deviation but social hierarchy in some form seems essential to mankind. Humans have the longest period of raising children of any species on the planet, so even the family is a source of centralized power, although it is not as ineffective as most centralized governments. While we depend on centralized power, it can be a source of ineffectiveness that gives an entry point for other forms of deviation.

The Third Principle
of Economic Actualism: Confusion

The first and second principle, uncertainty and certain deviation, can combine to make nominal economic data differ from actuality. Much confusion results from this discrepancy, and conflict can often be seen as a result of the confusion between nominal and actual economic reality. This confusion can become uncontrollable when social feedback mechanisms meant to keep economic deviation in line are hindered.

CONFUSION FROM UNCERTAINTY

The supply and demand of even the most free economies are shaped by the assumptions of the business cycle, by the duress and silent consent of the population. Economic transactions occur by the intersection of supply and demand curves as shown in Figure 8 below.

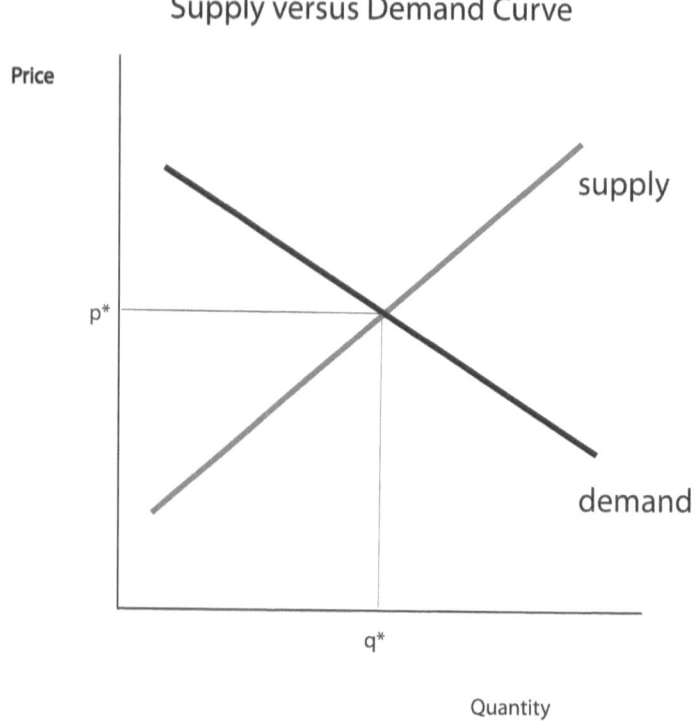

Figure 8 A graph showing a generalized supply curve against a generalized demand curve whose intersection determines the price (p*) and the quantity (*q) at equilibrium

Economic demand decreases as price increases. Supply increases as price increases. The two curves intersect to determine a price as is shown in Figure 8. Many economists believe that this mechanism works best when it is not interfered with by central bodies, and economic actualism gives credence to this belief.

Intervention by central figures often leads to economic problems such as undersupply in the long run. And economic actualism lists dependence upon centralized institutions as a source of economic deviation.

Some form of governance is always required. We can never be certain what the unimpeded worth of a transaction is. The supply and demand curves actually exist, but are shifted by social customs and law. The social conventions of the time weed out the endless possibilities for the supply and demand curves, and give us a single set of curves, and an economic transaction. The act of measuring an economic transaction with the assumptions, customs and currency of that economy, changes the outcome of that transaction.

Some governance of an economic transaction is inevitable. Consider an automobile. While the demand curve decreases as price increases, some people would prefer to get it free by stealing. And while supply increases as price increases, manufacturers are not allowed to simply not pay their suppliers for parts this month if last month's car did not sell. Economic transactions require customs and laws so that supply and demand curves, and economic transactions, form. Yet as we discussed in the first principle, no currency is perfect. Free and fair agreement is not universal and often consent is that of silence or duress. Participation in the whole of an economy is often motivated by a single product, such as a home. Having been forced to pay hundreds of thousands or even millions of dollars for a home, and being then forced to accept a job miles away to pay for it, the decision to spend thousands for a car becomes a relatively minor, even impulsive decision. The demand curve for transportation, in this instance, is set by the societal demands regarding housing. But these issues, perhaps because they are overwhelming as opposed to being insignificant, are unlikely to dominate the conversation during the car purchase or salesmanship.

The process of perfecting a currency is a constant work of feedback. Culturally, legally, politically and socially, we constant try to determine the best customs, habits, laws and regulations to modify economic and social transactions. We all recognize this, though we seldom speak about it. When we purchase an item, we are also purchasing a whole set of products and customs associated with that economy.

This lack of essential discussion causes confusion. A social impetus exists to persuade society that its currency is perfect, perhaps due to fear of other currencies. But each business cycle exists through consent. A busy complex society can not tolerate constant dickering over the ethics of minor and numerous transactions. Free and fair agreement is assumed, even when the consent is that of duress or silence. The assumption of free and fair agreement is a constant, invasive lie from which there seems no escape until the business cycle changes and another set of customs comes in as a replacement.

To change business cycles peacefully and smoothly, numerous social mechanisms exist to provide feedback to economic transactions. While barter may not exist in an actual transaction, society is a constant exchange of bartering over beliefs and conditions which help keep nominal economic status and actual economic status congruent. The forms of deviation between nominal and economic status which are most dangerous are those forms of deviation which interfere with these feedback mechanisms.

DEVIATION AND FEEDBACK

Economic deviation occurs as a change in nominal economic status causes a change in the opposite direction of actual economic status. This would be bad enough, however economic deviation becomes most destructive when it damages the economic feedback systems of a society, allowing the forces of confusion to grow without impediment.

An economy can be analogized to an electronic control system. A price is set by the intersection of a supply and demand curve under the rules of a business cycle. A change occurs. It could be anything: a depletion of resources or satisfaction of demand are examples. Under free market forces, one of the curves will move and the new nominal price will emerge as well as a new actual value. As we have seen, the customs of the business cycle will effect both the nominal value and the actual value and these customs are determined by tradition and a slew of social mechanisms.

Nominal and actual values can really diverge however, when a factor of economic deviation damages the social feedback mechanisms which we rely on to keep nominal and actual values aligned. In electronic control theory, control variables are mapped on graphs which are described by mathematical formulae. Systems can become unstable and blow up however when one portion of the graph involves division by zero. Since any number divided by zero is infinity or undefined, a mathematical control graph which has a portion of division by zero is unstable, since the system will become unstable and explode, either literally or actually, when the system operates in this range. The uninformed operator may never know the reason for the catastrophe and becomes doomed to repeat the accident.

Feedback destroying economic deviation has a similar effect. When certain social activities occur, feedback can create a loop where an increase in nominal wealth causes a decrease in actual wealth, which causes an increase in nominal wealth and a further decrease in actual wealth and so on and so on while it also disables social feedback mechanisms. This is similar to the failure of safety devices such as relief valves in an electronic control system. Disastrous confusion is the result. The deviation is an element which destroys actual value while increasing nominal value. This is dangerous enough. However, social feedback mechanisms which are meant to identify this process and correct for it are hindered or destroyed. This allows the economic deviation to grow unchecked and the instability of the social systems feeds on itself in an uncontrolled fashion. The business cycle spins out of control and can create all manner of social ills until it needs to be replaced, often through a violent process of war, rebellion, actual poverty or depression.

Much of this social confusion is best studied under the science of psychology as well as economics. Economic participation, particularly in a modern economy, demands the repressions of many needs and beliefs into the subconscious on a constant basis. Social communication, even in the form of "B" style horror genre cinema, deals with these repressed impulses. Political movements, commercial art, even coffee shop conversations between friends can also help people deal with these repressed issues. But without some sort of relief mechanism, these issues can create great confusion that threatens all of us as in the previously mentioned forms of economic deviation.

EXTERNALITIES AND FEEDBACK

Externalities are economic effects which are not recorded by the nominal statistics. However, most externalities can also affect the social feedback systems which are supposed to illuminate this diversion of actual and nominal economic status.

Environmental Issues

Destruction of the environment destroys feedback mechanisms in two main ways. It can damage alternate means of production, especially on the local scale. This increases commitment to a business cycle even when that business cycle diminishes actual wealth. As a factory spews pollution which destroys cropland, the local farmers may be forced to turn to the factory for employment, which drives down that factory's labour costs in a vicious cycle.

A second means by which environmental damage can destroy feedback mechanisms is by effecting individual and social health. Social feedback requires healthy and intelligent citizenry. A society which is injured by pollution either physically or mentally is less able to engage in the feedback mechanism which questions the diversion of nominal and actual wealth. The increasing evidence of dementia may be an upcoming example of this process in North America. Up to 50 % of 85 year olds in North America may have some form of dementia. But the increasing prevalence of Alzheimer's and related diseases decreases the resources of society to deal with social problems while increasing the nominal wealth created by a thriving retirement home industry. While we should be looking to our elderly as a source of wisdom, environmental health issues can make them a drain on the process of social discussion. Traces of pharmaceutical metabolites and hormone altering chemicals in our food have undetermined mental effects on a society.

Spirituality

The actual spiritual wealth of people and of a society can deviate from the nominal wealth of a society or an individual. Yet as spiritual wealth declines, so does the ability to provide social feedback and analysis. A society obsessed with instant gratification of artificially created demand can lose its intellectual focus. Societies without spiritual wealth can become mindless running on a treadmill after nothing, generating immense nominal wealth but little actual wealth yet without the ability to see the actual loss.

Leisure

Social feedback mechanisms require that people have a certain amount of time away from the grindstone of a punch clock to actually experience life and analyze their society. A society which increases nominal wealth while decreasing actual wealth through the diminishment of leisure opportunities not only deviates economically, it destroys the social processes which would keep this deviation in check.

IDOLATRIES AND FEEDBACK

Problems with branding do not provide the vicious cycle of accelerated feedback failure other means of deviation do. But branding or idolatries can deviate nominal and actual economic status and are an inescapable aspect of human communication in a complex society. On a macroeconomic scale, one brand's loss is usually another brand's gain and while these brands may be a poor reflection of reality, the total effect is a mere diminishment of actual wealth, not an inversion. Improper branding is merely a social feedback means which is not working very well through poor communication and unethical salesmanship. But at this time it is not thought to have the same destabilizing effect of other means of deviation. While the misrepresentation of an idolatry can diminish feedback capacity, in a healthy society of open thought, another agent will be able to challenge this idolatry.

Our present society seems to have an illness in this respect though. Social processes which diminish the opportunities for proper branding would represent a feedback threat.

INEFFECTIVENESS AND FEEDBACK

Where externalities can affect the physical and mental ability to evaluate through feedback mechanisms, feedback mechanisms are also needed to help to promote effectiveness.

Financial Obligations

Financial obligations can destroy a society's ability to adapt its customs in an effective manner to align actual and nominal wealth. Even in a depression, where people have leisure, spiritual strength and a lack of environmental damage, if they are bound to each other in excessive financial obligations, the currency will not allow them to adapt to changing circumstances.

Debts show up as a great source of nominal wealth, because they are recorded activities while at the same time they destroy the feedback mechanisms which would question its data of nominal wealth. In 2016, the uncontrolled expansion of bad debts over recent history has created both liquidity problems and an inability of new business cycle creation.

Conflict

It is often said that truth is the first casualty of war, yet conflict can be a source of nominal economic growth as we have seen. Even if people have leisure and spirituality, if they sense that they are in a conflict the process of feedback can become perverted. During conflict, a decrease in the actual wealth of others is seen as a benefit. The more this actual wealth decreases, the better. This can damage feedback mechanisms.

A related problem is that of envy. In an environment of increasing nominal growth but decreasing actual growth, it can seem like the enemy is gaining while we are losing. Due to an interest in increasing consent to the currency, the social belief persists that the increase in nominal wealth is a win-win situation.

Meanwhile, an individual only sees that he and his kind are losing. He sees a win-lose situation where he is losing and his enemies are winning. It is quite possible that the situation is a lose-lose situation but the demand of creating acceptance of the currency can not admit this without going to a new business cycle.

The class conflict described by Marx was a major intellectual force of the 20th century and may, in some instances, be the result of this failure of the feedback mechanisms. The workers feel exploited by a system where the nominal wealth is great and their actual wealth is poor. The owners of capital likewise are disillusioned by claims of great nominal wealth compared to their sacrifices of risk, labour, commitment and skill and imagine great hordes of workers in a life of plenty. Due to claims of nominal wealth, both envy the other imagining a win-lose situation which is really closer to a lose-lose situation. Or perhaps, the situation of the economy is neutral-neutral but the perceived injustice and resulting conflict converts it into a lose-lose situation.

Dependence on Centralization

As an economy becomes more dependent upon centralized institutions or foreign trade, the effect of meaningful social feedback can be diminished. In the centralizing institution's eyes, nominal growth is increasing actual growth. Their income often consists of a percentage of recorded nominal growth, in the form of taxes. Yet centralization can place issues upon central decision makers which they have neither the ability nor the motivation to resolve. You can write a congressman until you are blue in the face about the many issues you are dealing with, only to find that he has even more issues going across his desk than you do. Centralization can overburden the demands of democracy onto a few, even if they were voted in. This centralization is inescapable to some extent yet it leads to other deviations.

With advances in media technology, such as film, print or television, the process of communication itself can create dependence on centralization. Communication is a central aspect of social feedback which can be destroyed by this form of economic deviation.

Prevention of Damage and Error

These forms of economic deviation confuse nominal with actual wealth but do not destroy feedback unless they reach extreme levels of communication or societal breakdown.

RESULTING CONFUSION

Discussion and debate are required for effective economic transactions to ensure customs of the business cycle are appropriate. And economic transactions are essential to life. But uncertainty is the result of duress and silent consent. And economic deviation is certain to create nominal wealth at the expense of actual poverty and actual wealth at the expense of nominal poverty. Sometimes this deviation destroys social feedback mechanisms making it uncontrollable.

These problems not only necessitate social debate, they are usually the underlying subject of conversation in one way or another. Differentiating nominal and actual wealth in these discussions can help bring subjects into focus.

The problems of uncertainty are most difficult to deal with since we are never sure they are actually occurring. Transparency is a frequent goal of the information age. But the overabundance of information can be as much of a problem as the lack of information. We like to think that the era of public corporations are transparent and no uncertainty exists, but the financial crisis of 2008, and other crises, persuades us that this is not so.

Deviation is certain to occur and the direction of its deviation is usually predictable, but the amount is hard to estimate. However, the process of deviation can actually destroy the feedback mechanisms which keep the deviation in check, resulting in confusion.

ECONO-ADDICTION

The practice of increasing nominal wealth is not necessarily bad. It is only when increasing nominal wealth decreases actual wealth that problems can arise, especially as the feedback mechanisms that keep deviation in check are destroyed.

However, the situation can progress where individuals or a society become obsessed with the increase of nominal wealth, even at the expense of actual wealth. It is essential to first consider the enormity of nominal economic growth. A conservative estimate of nominal economic growth is one percent a year. In recent years, China has grown at close to ten percent. But we can consider a one percent growth rate of the economy since the dawn of civilization, about six thousand years ago. We can compound this interest rate of one percent to the power of six thousand on a simple calculator just as in interest calculations:

$1.01^{6000} = 6.48 * 10^{25}$

However, it may have only been 4000 years since civilization was destroyed in a great flood such as Noah's flood. If we take this formula from 4000 years we get:

$1.01^{4000} = 1.03 * 10^{17}$

However, the world's population has grown from a very small sample, say "one" for ease of computation, to 7 billion in the last four thousand years. If we divide the amount that the nominal economy has grown by the growth in the human population we get:

$1.03*10^{17} / 7*10^{9} = 20.6$ million

These calculations approximate that the average human has a nominal wealth that is twenty million times that of a man from the dawn of civilization. This may seem like an absurd figure, but consider the consumption of fish from the second principle. If someone caught a fish with his bare hands, he eats the fish but there is very little nominal growth. As he makes a spear, the spear counts as nominal growth. Hooks and the infrastructure to produce them create more nominal growth, as do nets. Wagons and small boats to get to new fishing

Introducing Economic Actualism

grounds create new nominal wealth. Then huge trawlers, with built-in refrigeration and navigation create a nominal wealth that is millions of times that of a person's bare hands to get the same actual wealth: a fish for consumption. The North American fishing market has followed this decline from the private consumption of freshwater fish, to the collapsing Newfoundland cod industry to huge sonar equipped vessels that scour the remote regions of the earth's seas for progressively smaller fish.

Science fiction could postulate about another astronomical increase in the nominal wealth to catch fish in the future. A comet's water 3,000 years from now could be diverted to provide

© Tom Eagan - Dreamstime.com

Figure 9 As fishing resources have become more scarce on a local basis the nominal size of the industry has continued to grow, outsizing the actual increase in the world wide actual harvest which has lately decreased.

water and atmosphere to the moon, creating a lunar aquaculture industry which would send frozen fish back to a polluted earth. It sounds crazy, and it is. But if future generations could pull something like that off, the nominal growth would be spectacular, while the actual growth would be minimal. The present fishing industry would have seemed like incredible science fiction to ancient society, and a little crazy.

This extra work and cost of a globalized fishing industry would seem like a bad thing. Yet to people manufacturing hooks, nets, freezers, boats and GPS systems, this growth is a source of wealth. To governments, this recorded activity can be taxed as a source of revenue. To bankers, many of whom are economists, the infrastructure of modern fishing equipment is an opportunity for loan agreements.

The nominal growth of a modern economy can be astronomically higher compared to an actual growth which is stagnant, or even declining. Yet actual growth can be hard to account for, and many business men, governments and economists have a vested interest in obsessing on nominal records, since this is a source of income. Without a method to find the actual within the nominal, assessing the change in actual wealth can seem like an overwhelming array of ill-defined possibilities.

Many times, it seems like the more actual wealth declines, the more people cling to the hope of growing nominal wealth. Nominal wealth can seem certain and true because it is recorded, while actual wealth becomes an increasing mystery. Psychology definitely has a play, with both rational and irrational aspects playing a role. As Freud saw repressed sex playing a role in psychiatry in German society of the early 1900's, repressed anger and fears about decreasing actual wealth and uncertainty about the insecurity of nominal wealth are a common source of anxiety.

The New Testament says that for we can not serve both God and "Mammon" (Matthew 6:24), which is often translated as God and "money". It also says that for the love of money, many men will pierce themselves with many sorrows (1Timothy 6:10).

This love of money may be seen as a love of nominal wealth, for God does not want us to suffer poverty that would drive us from him.

In the last hundred years, our love of money has subjected mankind's society to many self-inflicted troubles. Our politicians flirt with communism, fascism, anarchy in the financial community, anything to keep the nominal economy growing until the inevitable collapse of the business cycle leads to a confused poverty and angst. Applying actualism to determine the forces separating nominal from actual wealth can provide a guiding framework. It is a common sense approach to give common sense answers to real problems.

Not all econo-addiction is an intentional act. It is best to think of econo-addiction as a continuum between intentional and non-intentional econo-addiction. All of us are addicted to nominal growth to a certain extent. Without econo-addiction, we do not get paid. There may be a few central bankers who are more aware of the growing difference between nominal and actual wealth. But these people may also be most removed from the actual wealth, as their world consists of financial statements, and can be removed from data about actual wealth.

Understanding and patience will be required to bring the economy back to actual wealth. The first step to dealing with econo-addiction is to realize that the answer to econo-addiction is not more nominal growth, any more than the solution to heroin addiction is more heroin, a violent opinion of many addicts. A plan is necessary, and it is believed the best way to develop such a plan is to apply the described prospects of economic actualism in a systematic manner, particularly with the consideration of diminishing returns. On the macroeconomic scale, this process will be subject to controversy and political debate, but this debate is a required aspect in the improvement of an economy.

The good news is also that a decline in nominal wealth is not necessarily a decline in actual wealth. Many people panic during periods of recession. Yet as we have seen, the nominal wealth of modern man may be 20.6 million times the nominal wealth of ancient man, while the increase of actual wealth has been much less. There is opportunity here! The decrease in nominal wealth during a recession may be an increase in the actual wealth, affording new opportunities with reduced conflict, more spirituality and leisure, fewer externalities and less error and more opportunity for the profits of appropriate feedback. Economic actualism, and we are all part "actualist" even if we do not use the word, can help us to seize the day even when the nominalist viewpoint, and we are all partly nominalist, seems bleak.

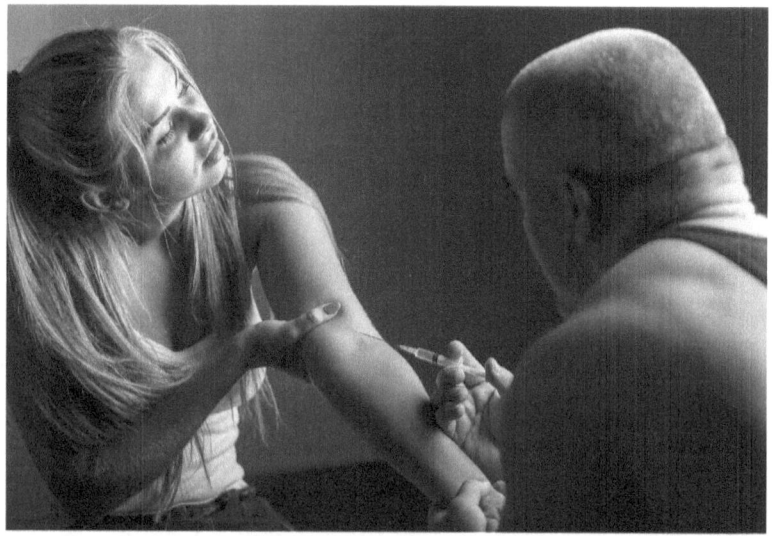

©Artemfurman – Dreamstime.com

Figure 10 To some people, the only solution to drug addiction is more of that drug. Not seeing this drug as a potential danger is a red flag that the drug problem is serious. Yet many of us refuse to see a hazard in econo-addiction

Introducing Economic Actualism

© Rohappy – Dreamstime.com

Figure 11 Decreases in nominal wealth can yield opportunities to increase actual wealth. But just as acquiring nominal wealth requires care and skill, so does acquiring actual wealth.

Finding actual wealth within social relationships is essential to existence and a constant, though usually non-verbalized, effort for all of us. It is also an unspoken thread throughout intellectual history, in a diversity of disciplines. Human intelligence is burdened with the need to balance both the actual and the nominal world and this struggle has had effects on every avenue of our thought over thousands of years of our civilization.

Economic actualism is largely an application of analytical philosophy to economics. "Actualism" is the name of a branch of analytical philosophy developed in the later 1900's to look at how some realities are actual while others are only possible or fictitious. Economic actualism has been developed independently but it shares a similar goal of looking at relationships between the actual and the possible, except that it looks at existence economically.

This book is primarily about economics. But as economics strives to describe rational behaviour, or how we should behave, it serves as a cornerstone in the housing of our intellectuality and has vital links to other sciences, particularly the social sciences. This book is the first in a series of books that explore our struggle to live in both the actual and the nominal world with its social representations.

Our psychology, our philosophy, our religions like Christianity which is perhaps the earliest developed expression of economic actualism, our theology, our politics and our art all struggle with this problem. Yet as we progress with this problem, it will relieve bottlenecks in our science while it relives burdens in our lives in a variety of ways. We can seize the day by using opportunities that avail themselves outside of the economy or we can modify our economic participation to yield more actual rewards by reducing duress, increasing effectiveness, mitigating inversions, seeking icons and relating better to other actors as we improve our own participation. The opportunities are multiple, various, major and enticing.

Chapter Two

Certain Deviation

Some economic deviation is certain to occur. You can count on it. In an economy, only three things are certain to occur: death, taxes and economic deviation. It is unavoidable that nominal wealth will increase as a result of a decrease in actual wealth. This is called "the second principle" of economic actualism since "the first principle" of uncertainty is more essential. However, the first principle is also harder to grasp and has more of a psychological aspect. It is described more in my book "The Psychology of Economic Actualism". It is easier to understand the first principle after studying the second principle, so the second principle is listed here first.

Economic deviation is dangerous. It is like having a reverse speedometer on your car so that when you speed up you think you are slowing down and when you slow down you think you are speeding up. While no one would tolerate a car that drives like this, most of us tolerate economic deviation with reckless abandon. Business cycles rise and fall as their nominal status becomes attractive to people, who participate but neglect to account for the deviation from actual wealth until eventually, the deviation of nominal data from actual reality becomes too great.

People then begin to leave the business cycle and it declines to be replaced by another set of nominal measures. Many a life has become a fatality due to the resulting economic accident and entire societies have collapsed because their nominal wealth told them they were prospering while their actual wealth declined. Their records of nominal wealth were an inversion of actual reality. They found themselves trapped by these inversions without choice. Wars, depressions, stock market crashes, unemployment and revolutions can occur during the change from one business cycle to another.

Monitoring the deviation between nominal and actual economic data is essential to understanding an economy and its participants. Perceiving the difference between actual and nominal economic wealth is also essential in an individual's life. It can mean the difference between being rich and being happy. Or it can mean the difference between being free and living a life you can not stand. But you have to be active with it. You must try to perceive between the presentations of nominal value placed before you and their actual worth. Everywhere you look, members of the economy will try to sell you that their good or service is an indisputable source of actual wealth.

DEVIATION FROM IDOLATRY

Idolatry is unlike other forms of deviation. It creates an unnatural nominal value for one item. Because it does this without changing the total economic output of the set of goods and services under consideration, it forces the nominal values of other items to balance in the opposite direction. One man's beauty is another man's trash and great resources of time have been spent over the years to create perceptions in the marketplace than an item has unnaturally high value, only in time to have the actual value revealed.

Perhaps one of the most famous examples of economic idolatry is the tulip craze of 1637. One discovery from the first ships to India was the tulip. And when bulbs for the ornamental flowers were brought back to Holland the beauty of their spring time blooms became a rage. To have tulips in your garden was a mark of distinction. Over time, breeding was successful in creating even more distinctive tulips which carried more prestige and commanded higher prices. Having tulips became a necessity for a home owner much as having a well-kept lawn was deemed essential for the middle class of 1950's United States of America.

Over about forty years the price of tulips kept rising until speculation occurred. People saw the prices were rising and, afraid of being "left out" invested in tulip bulbs in the belief that their nominal value would continue to rise, invested in the bulbs without thought of the tulip bulbs actual value. Speculation inflated tulip prices. Eventually, you could buy a good building lot on waterfront Amsterdam with a single tulip bulb and then, suddenly, the market for tulip bulbs collapsed. Even a slight dip in the price of tulips caused an end to the speculation of endless nominal price rises and suddenly, the substantially lower actual value raised the spectre of speculation about price decreases, which lead to a rapid lowering of prices. But, like in many business cycles, fortunes were made and lost on this business cycle. Those who got in early with the tulip bulb supply were made fabulously wealthy, while those who bought in at the end lost everything they invested.

The early spice trade was a concurrent business cycle that made some spectacularly wealthy. A ship that left Holland and returned with a load of spices yielded returns of twenty times that which was invested, more than enough to pay for the many ships which were lost at sea due to storms or mutiny. But unlike the tulip bulbs, these spices had actual lasting value in that they could be used to make inferior food taste more palatable. Also, unlike the tulips, the spices could not be regenerated in the cooler climate of northern Europe and so the business cycle was not as easy to replace. So while, over centuries, the price of spices did fall, the business cycle for spices was much longer and the decline more gradual than that of the tulip bulb. The market for tulips proved to be much more idolatrous than the market for spices, but at the time, many investors, did not realize this. Tulips came to idolize that excitement of Europe's colonial age. Tulip bulbs symbolized the virtues of the world exploration of that time, but had little of the actual lasting benefits.

Products or services develop into idols when their nominal wealth, or perceived wealth, exceeds their actual wealth and this excess can often grow exponentially without control only to collapse just as suddenly. These idols gain excessive value because they exemplify the excitement of their culture. The tulip was new in

© Neirfy – Dreamstime.com

Figure 12 Nearly 400 years after the tulip craze swept through the economy of Holland, tulips still hold a prominent position in Dutch culture.

Europe at the time of the Tulip Craze and it was a visual example of the exciting variety of new plants which the exploration of the world promised was delivering. So while it had no essential value of its own, the emotion of the time gave it value according to the non-discriminating impulses of the time.

Another example from the same era would be the investment in the City of New Orleans in pre-revolutionary France of the 1700's. The exploration of the new world produced riches in gold which were unknown at the time and people were selling shares in corporations which were exploiting the new world. Those who got in on the ground floor of these stocks made fortunes that were the envy of others. But investors had to wait for at least a couple of years from when a ship set sail until it returned with its reports. Speculation ran rampant and investors bankrupted the country with their speculations. In the end a rumour went around that New Orleans, Louisiana was a huge gold deposit and the government and the economy collapsed from excessive belief in these gold riches. Louisiana had a lot going for it but gold was not one of them. The Louisiana gold was paper gold only, no physical gold existed. But people still gave it value. This gold fervour got the better of both aristocracy and government while John Law, the man at the heart of the first French stock market, fled the country.

WHAT MAKES AN IDOL?

The tulip of the early 1600's and Louisiana gold of the 1700's were both idols that acquired immense nominal values with minimal, even non-existent, actual values. They were major trends in the culture of their time. The majority of the population attributed nominal value to them, so they had nominal value which people could exchange for actual wealth. Idols are a made from a combination of perceived scarcity, perceived durability and representativeness.

Even in the twenty-first century gold is an idol in itself, both as paper gold and as physical gold. Physical gold symbolizes many skills that men admire such as mining, durability, beauty and security. It has a splendour and immortality that makes it easy to market for jewellery and investment. People like gold. It has economic value as well. It is an excellent conductor of heat and electricity and is very malleable. But the desire of men for gold exceeds its physical attributes for three reasons: its perceived distinctiveness, its perceived lasting scarcity and its representation of worthy attributes. The perceived scarcity creates a perceived lack of supply and perceptions of distinctiveness create demand. Representation hinders feedback.

Whereas regular products satisfy a real need such as wheat satisfying hunger, an idol serves as a representation of other products which meets a demand. This is crucial to the creation of an idol because representation allows for the hindrance of feedback mechanisms which prevent idols from forming. When a product meets an immediate demand, its value is instantly appraised. But when a product is representative of an attribute only, appraisal is less effective. To acquire an unreasonably high nominal value, a product must be representative of some attribute people are excited about. These three ingredients: distinctiveness, perceived lasting scarcity and representation can combine to make an idol. And idols come in many forms.

Take the tulip for example: The tulip was, and still is, a distinctive flower. You can spot a red tulip against green grass from a hundred yards away and nothing else, to this day, looks quite like it. To the layman, most other spices and their plants look fairly similar. Ground cinnamon looks rather like ground cumin from one hundred yards away, even less than that. And cinnamon bark looks rather like the bark of a skinny red twig, nothing that would evoke emotion. But the tulip represented the wonders of the early spice trade at the time. It was a new plant from one of the faraway lands with

Introducing Economic Actualism

their new era of promise. Potatoes, for instance, were in many ways the plant that allowed for the population explosion in Europe during the 1600's as it was a high calorie per acre crop which could grow in the cold climate of Northern Europe. Its importation as a new crop from South America was a marvel at the time. The distinctive tulip, as the most visual of the new crops, represented the wonders of all the new crops. The tulip satisfied no immediate need such as hunger, taste or medicine. So appraisal of its actual worth was delayed.

But where the tulip failed as a lasting idol was in its perceived lasting scarcity. Unlike many spices the tulip could be seeded and grown in northern Europe. This was masked for decades as people kept breeding new varieties of tulip, each of which was scarce for a while but was replaced by another new variety. The spiral of scarcity kept continuing as original varieties of tulips were replace by newer, more distinctive and exotic varieties until, eventually, none of the new tulips were scarce any more. People bred the bulbs and flooded the market. Without scarcity, you can not maintain the value of an idol in a free market place.

Gold however, has been an idol that has lasted through the millennia. It is distinctive. The layman can easily recognize its yellow and beautiful hue. While platinum, which is rarer, looks rather like any of the other numerous silver coloured metals. Gold represents the wealth of mining and man's ingenuity in his exploitation of nature. It is always rare. It is only $3.1*10^{-7}\%$ of the earth's crust and while it has lasting value, it is very durable and never corrodes. The newly mined gold never seems to totally flood the market. Diamonds are a similar idol in that they are distinctive, rare, and representative. However, it has yet to be seen if the manufacture of artificial diamonds will allow for their continued scarcity.

It is important to note that no one has the ability to absolutely determine whether a good or service is, in that present economy, an idol. Though many central planners would like the power to set prices, like all humans, they are liable to error. It is easy for us in retrospect, to look at the tulip crisis and say that the market of that time and place created an idol. We would like to think if we were alive then, that we would have recognized the situation. But hindsight is 20/20, especially in market prediction. For every buyer, there is a seller, trying to convince him that the price is reasonable.

A VARIETY OF IDOLS

It is not a matter of if idols exist in a society but what idols exist in a society, and to what extent. Idolatry is an inescapable outcome of human interaction. Human economic interaction requires branding. Whether it be Og the Caveman, who makes the best spears or Ramses the pharaoh of ancient Egypt, who has divine authority, social stratification requires brands to communicate true value. And where ever you have brands to communicate true value you inevitably get idols that communicate mistaken value. As people communicate error, either purposely or mistakenly, they create idols. As this idolatry increases nominal value of the idols value, it decreases the nominal value of other products in the set which is being considered.

Many goods become idols such as fancy houses, luxury cards or cool clothes. They can come to symbolize status rather than filling a direct need. Other worthy attributes that can be symbolized are sex appeal, health, rebellion against the establishment, beauty, wisdom; the list goes on. Distinctiveness of goods is a key component of product design. Color or appearance can be enough. But often a unique feature can be a sales tool as well, though features are likely to be less representational than style or color. Perception of scarcity can be produced through real restriction of supply.

Services can represent the same attributes as goods can. Some people, who are able to afford it, hire servants for the prestige. And most people who successfully market services will try to give themselves a marketable image, such as that of professionalism. However, the effects of most services are fairly immediate. Since most services are not durable in the way that some goods are durable goods, they are less susceptible to representation and are less likely to form idols.

Locales and institutions always have a history that they represent and are often marketed on the basis of that history. The fact that this history is primarily the product of previous residents, who have usually long since departed, does not negate the emotional impact which these histories create. Locations create idols, as do institutions. Our culture revels in the idolatry of certain post-secondary educational institutions. And this revelry often attracts people based on the promoted history to maintain the idol.

In real estate, the same effect also happens to a lesser degree. Land ownership has immediate discernable benefits and is less subject to representation than institutions. While many businesses, at least most traditional businesses, have values based upon assets and earnings with little room for idolatry, this is not always the case and many companies and their trademarks gain idolatrous values. All of these idols are subject to feedback.

Celebrities are often idols, perhaps by definition. For they allow us to "celebrate" some worthy attribute which seems to be in scarce supply. To many high school students, rock stars idolize rebellion and a counter culture. Movie stars allow fans to celebrate the personae of their screen performances. Politicians often idolize the ideologies they represent. And all leaders, who wish to lead by example, must nurture their own image. People often thrive or fail due to the intangible effects of their own distinctiveness and how well they represent their own worthy attributes.

Currencies are perhaps most vulnerable to idolatries. Most currency has no tangible value of its own. Its value comes solely from the other products and services which it represents. To maintain its value it must generate a perception of sustained scarcity and appear distinctive, as if it alone has the distinct status as the legal tender for its jurisdiction.

Certain events become idols because they symbolize the culture and people of a time and place. "Woodstock", for example, has gained a legendary status as the music concert that defined the baby boom generation of the United States of America. Even the name "Woodstock" evokes emotions and memories to those of that generation. In contrast, the name "Auschwitz" also evokes memories and emotions to those who lived in the twentieth century, but those emotions and memories are of an entirely different nature.

In the present reality, both of these sites are relatively unoccupied fields with similar grass and flowers blooming in each site. Yet the attributes which they represent make them totally different types of idols. Modern media has an ability to make idols from events which the media of previous ages have not had and which modern society has seemed to be ill prepared for.

However, the most invasive form of idolatry is words themselves. Words are symbols, and they are prone to error. To symbolize an object in your kitchen as a "plate" as opposed to a "platter" or "tray" or "dish" or "coaster" may not seem crucial. But some words have more consequences when used incorrectly.

Words like "criminal" or "lover" can be damaging when used inappropriately. For all of us have done something illegal, whether it was parking our car incorrectly, smoking pot or jaywalking. But we would object to being defined as "criminals" on this basis. And if we did not object, the label would be damaging. Likewise the socially minded amongst us try to "love" everyone we know, but to claim at a cocktail party that we were "lovers" with someone who was happily married to another would be disastrous. "Slander" and "libel" laws provide some protection against extreme errors, but the correct use of language is a life long struggle. Error in the use of words can create great social stress to both speaker and audience. To avoid this spiritual strife, many eastern and western monks through the ages have taken vows of silence as a means of spiritual growth. Yet the rest of us poor mortals are condemned to a constant struggle in the use of words as symbols, just as we deal with other forms of idolatries in our hectic lives.

UNNATURAL BARGAINS

We commonly think of idols as raising the price of an object but the process of idolatry can lower the value of goods and services as well with results that are equally disastrous. An idol is created by perceived distinctiveness, perceived lasting scarcity and representation of worthiness. In the formation of an unnatural bargain, the economic price of an object can be unreasonably lowered by the opposite: perceived commonness, perceived lasting abundance and representation of unworthiness. This can be very destructive.

Perhaps one of the best examples of unnatural bargains was that of colonialism: a system and accompanying set of philosophies which previous generations, primarily in Europe, fell into that resulted in great destruction across the globe; a very ineffective, and many would say unjust, means of economic consumption. Colonialism can lead to depressed prices which result in destruction of natural resources. Colonialism can philosophically take a diverse population and render them basically homogenous, robbing them of their perceived distinctiveness. This lack of distinctiveness could label the numerous indigenous societies of North Americans as "savages" to expedite consumption to feed a ravenous Europe without having to deal with a whole lot of distinct "societies". It even labelled them with the term "Indian" after a country most of them had probably never heard of and had no interest in.

But we all have a bad habit of reducing distinctiveness for the ease of communication. I have done this twice already in this book and you may have found it to be mildly annoying. Earlier, I referred to the cod fish as being basically the same as fish caught now in the South Pacific. This was a decision made from a teaching viewpoint. From the endpoint of the consumer, I know of no essential difference between the cod of the North Atlantic and the numerous species of diverse fish in the South Pacific. While I am sure some taste a little different, or have a slightly different fat content, it was irrelevant to the point I was trying to make. I imagine that there is at least one fish in the South Pacific that is poisonous. And even the word "cod" is a generalization as there are different types of fish that have been or are classified as cod. Within the cod population, each fish in each distinct school is a distinct individual amongst themselves, though to us they all look very similar.

The cod may have a distinct place in the ecology of the North Atlantic that is hard to fill in the South Pacific, but unfortunately we have consumed most of the cod without determining their distinctive ecological role. Marine biologists are presently trying to determine this role, but it is hard to analyze a dead ecosystem. The earlier passage was a description of economic principles, not marine biology however. So I neglected the distinctiveness of the cod since it was not essential to the topic at hand.

Likewise earlier in this chapter, I said the grasses and flowers of "Woodstock" and "Auschwitz" were similar. From a realtor's point of view, this may be the case. But the assumption that the fauna of different continents are the same robs them of the distinctiveness that they have. Again, the biological distinctiveness was not relevant to the conversation. Such decisions about when an aspect of distinctiveness is pertinent to the conversation are inescapable aspects of communication.

Introducing Economic Actualism

Every word we use is a symbol and a potential idol. But when we decide that the distinctiveness of the object is irrelevant, we cheapen it. Fostering a perception of lasting abundance lowers a price too. Just as communication inevitably raises the risk of discounting distinctiveness, so haggling constantly raises the spectre of exaggerating the supply and permanence of a good.

Colonialism is justified by promoting the belief that the resources of the subject country are inexhaustible. Be they fish, trees, arable lands, buffalo, or diverse species, the human race is realizing that over the last few centuries colonialism has gobbled up much of the 4 billion year old planet without securing alternative resources. The cod of the North Atlantic were reported to be populous enough in 1497 by John Cabot to feed mankind until the "end of the world". But the fish are gone and the world lives on.

Representation of unworthiness also lowers values unnecessarily. When colonialism does represent the distinctiveness of foreign populations it often represents them as differing varieties of "uncivilized" and so devalues them. Many native cultures have entirely, or almost entirely, disappeared. The process of idolatry can either inflate the value of something or deflate the value. However, when it is idolatry the price change is balanced by an opposite action in the set of consideration. The set of consideration is the group of items under concern. It could be a household budget, the resources of an industry's research and development, a government department's annual budget, or the nominal and actual resources of an entire country. Depending upon your defined set of consideration, many things could be idolatrous.

When colonialism deflates the value of foreign land it exaggerates the value of the colonizer's power within a global set of consideration. When natural resources such as fish stocks are devalued, fishing boats and coastal villages are inflated in value and also, the value of people living in those communities increases in value until the resource is depleted. When a car brand is inflated in value, its competitors will lose value.

Many people don't realize this balancing of inflated and deflated values because economists typically deal with a narrow range of phenomenon, that which is monetarily recorded. Like all forms of communication, economic data itself falls victim to idolatry. Thus inflating the value of "employed" people devalues the work of other forms of labour such as housework. Inflation of real estate prices is balanced by the devaluation of homeless people. Inflations in the number of people being "educated" devalues the amount of other forms of learning. People can have many valuable learning experiences outside of school. Whenever one thing is raised improperly above its worth, the rest of society in general, or maybe a few items in particular is lowered though often the lowering is hard to quantify. We can assume that overall, it is a zero sum gain as far as idolatry is concerned, and that is the danger of idolatry. Deciding what items fall into the set of consideration is political.

MODERN TRENDS OF IDOLATRY

As the "economy" has grown, many things about society have changed and these changes have influenced the processes of idolatry. The three elements of distinctiveness, sustained scarcity and representativeness of worth still remain. Feedback to keep idolatry in check has become hampered by a number of issues. But it is important to note that nobody has an all seeing eye to judge on what has become an idol in our modern age. That is the objective of central planners which usually ends in disaster. But it is also imperative that we must try to determine the effects our modern society is having on the process. We will not be 100 percent correct in our efforts, but the effort must be made.

Distinctiveness is the aspect that best illustrates the zero sum gain principle. To be distinctive is not just to be different but uniquely worthy or uniquely unworthy. One unique item which gathers the eye of all for a short period renders everything else into obscurity. More than at any other time, our modern media has the ability to gather the attention of the multitude onto one item.

The obscurity of other items and issues, which may be more distinct, is the result. But the issue as to what quality people are looking at as distinctive is one of trends and varies from one class of goods to another. For manufactured goods, the distinctiveness is often innovation. A feature that is new in a product like a car makes the whole car seem better designed, manufactured and marketed. In products like food, new features can be distinctively bad as they conjure up images of chemical additives, genetic modification and food processing. "Natural" is often the distinctively good characteristic for food. Modern society seems to hold both "new" or "natural" up for distinction. "New" is distinctive because of the information age and the promise that it holds. While "natural" is distinctive because of the widespread influence of man's previous activities and invention. In the arts, "rebellion" is increasingly held up as distinctive as thousands of artists compete to be the most distinctively rebellious, all within the corporate and government structures which pay them of course. In an increasingly atheist media, religious figures who in the past were held as distinctive are now largely replaced by humanist figures. The list of qualities for which distinction is sought are as endless as there are target markets. The preceding are a few noted general trends but depending upon your own personal demographic characteristics, marketers will appeal to you on the basis of these and other qualities.

The actual issue of distinctiveness in a media age can be quite trite. Modern media has allowed the use of seemingly insignificant features to create significant distinctiveness. It has been a long time since Henry Ford said of his Model T automobile that "you can have any color you want as long as it is black". For a long time, the color of appliances was held up as a feature of distinction. Now, not so much. But many a celebrity gains distinction from the color of the clothing, hair or make up.

The perception of lasting scarcity can come from organized market supply. Unions, marketing associations and guilds create shortage to increase their prices. Media can also be used to create the perception of prolonged scarcity, but this is subject to the message from other voices. But the main forces promoting idolatry from the modern age come from representativeness as the result of mankind's transition up Maslow's hierarchy combined with increasing complexity and new media.

Maslow's hierarchy is a psychological theory that people have a pyramid of needs or motivations with physiological needs as a base. When these are fulfilled they satisfy needs for safety. When those are fulfilled they satisfy needs for love and belonging. When those are fulfilled they satisfy needs for needs for esteem. And when esteems needs are met they satisfy needs for self-actualization: what man can be he must be, as Maslow says. Much of standard economic theory is based on the old capitalist belief that man's history is a process of mankind dominating the world of nature to feed, house and clothe himself. These theories worked better in those earlier societies than they do in modern societies, in part, because the goods at the base of Maslow's hierarchy are not as subject to representation. People know very quickly if they eat too little calories, or if they are cold or naked.

Idolatry is less of a problem with these basic needs than it is for higher level needs. And with each step up Maslow's hierarchy, the economy relies more on representation of worthiness and is more susceptible to idolatry. Those who live in the higher levels of Maslow's Pyramid, which is all of us to some extent, should be wary of idolatry. Maslow's pyramid is shown in Figure 13.

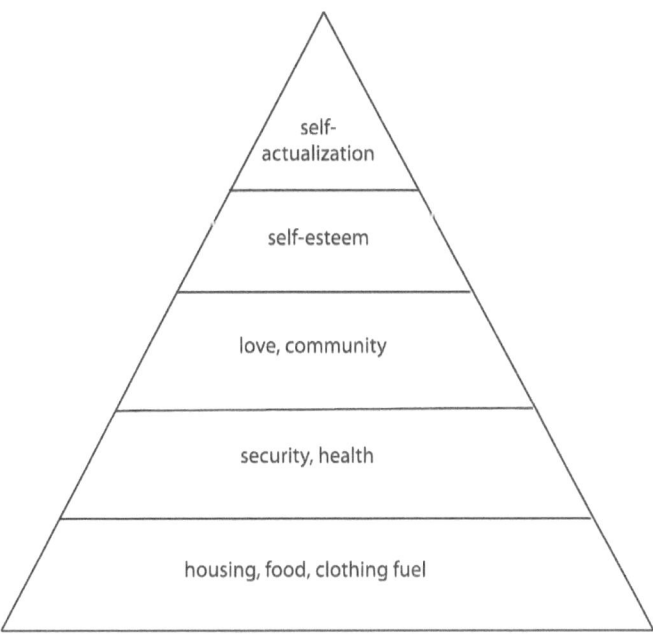

Figure 13. Maslow's Hierarchy of Needs postulates that needs for things like housing and food must be satisfied before a person will pursue long term health before they look for community, then self-esteem and then self-actualization, which is fulfilling your full potential.

After our needs for food, water, housing, and excrement are satisfied we look for security: physical security in the means of health, financial security and law. Health requires more representation than mere calorie consumption does as it is not always obvious what will lead to long term health but the satiation of hunger comes in about twenty minutes after a meal. The modern man struggles with various representations of which foods prevent heart disease and cancer, what is the best exercise regimen etc. The answers often are unclear. Likewise, we all struggle with questions of law and order. The first level of hierarchy is how to deal with a punch that has injured our physiological health. The second level is about how we create laws preventing fist fights. This requires legal representation as the answers are less clear.

Financial security is also less clear. Simply having bigger stacks of money in the bank is not always practical or sufficient.

Love and belonging is increasingly nebulous. The Beatles song says that "money can't buy me love" but people sure do try. Advertisements say we'll be popular if we buy this good or service. People purchase but no real answer ever materializes about whether the purchase was the reason for their love, and most would prefer to believe that the belonging is the result of the consumer's inner beauty rather than a purchase. Traditional economic theory assumes that people are rational, and so does economic actualism. For what could be more rational than the need to belong. But the search for love can easily cause nominal and actual values to drift apart since it requires representation, rather than direct feedback.

Esteem takes the level of representation up again, though it may be said that for many esteem is less nebulous than love. This may depend upon your discernment of esteem. For some, buying a new suit and tie may give esteem as a status symbol, whereas love can never be bought. But again representation is required. In later years (1970) Maslow introduced two new levels to his hierarchy here: cognitive needs and aesthetic needs. These are closely allied with esteem. Cognitive needs, that of knowing, can be met by buying books or schooling. But sometimes knowing "too much" is really "knowing nothing at all". Many admire the view from a tall skyscraper thinking they can see far away, but in this process of people appearing like ants they lose knowledge of the faces of those people. When our gaze is directed at one thing we lose sight of something else. Sometimes the most important thing to know is what comes from inside. We constantly see representations of what we should know.

Beauty is one form of self-esteem that is becoming a runaway system of economic growth as well. Young girls wrap their self-esteem by comparing their appearance to those on magazine covers, not realizing that the representations are of professional models who have been Photoshopped. Beauty is in the eye of the beholder. And these representations, while they are a source of exponential nominal growth, are not properly representing the actual economy.

If esteem is to see your own worth and to have others see it then self-actualization is to fulfill your own worth, to "be all that you can be". Very nebulous stuff with a lot of potential for idolatry, but it is also a step up on the Maslow hierarchy and very noble stuff. Of course, one person's worthy attributes will differ from another's. To one the attribute may be charity, to another self-control, another leadership, another athleticism. And people largely evaluate their self-actualization by comparing themselves to others. One who aspires to athleticism will evaluate himself well in a field that is less athletic and poorly if society's athletic ability improves. This level of Maslow's hierarchy may require economic investment, but the determination of actual economic progress is largely internal to the person. Yet he will be subject to the counsel of the economy's nominal representations.

In 1970 Maslow added a final level in the hierarchy, "transcendence", that of helping others meet their self-actualization. This is far removed from traditional economic theory because it is so dependent of representation, because the feedback of worth is so remote and because the feedback is dependent upon society's idolatries.

As people, and as our society, progress up Maslow's hierarchical pyramid we become further removed from direct economic feedback and become more prone to idolatry. The potential for difference between nominal economic data and actual economic reality increases. In the lower levels of Maslow, economic activity "sticks to the knitting" and life is predictable and secure. But as we migrate up the pyramid, we subject ourselves to financial insecurity, threatening our status on the second level of Maslow. When we go into debt to create esteem and self-actualization, we are threatening the security from the second level which our upper level activity relies upon. But debt alone is not the only threat. The process of idolatry can skew our perceptions in other ways. We must actively delineate the difference between nominalism and actual reality or the gain in our belonging, esteem, and self-actualism may be nothing than commercialized smoke and mirrors.

Complexity

Travelling up the Maslow pyramid does not necessarily increase the complexity of life. It just means that the complexity often associated with lower levels has been simplified, allowing us to explore the complexities of the upper Maslow levels. But the culture of modern life is thrusting complexity upon us regardless of what level we are concentrating upon. This complexity comes from two main sources: technology and globalism.

Technology is creating an information age. Where ancient man drank well and spring water without knowledge of its microbial content, he knew that some water was good and some bad and that was about as complex as it got. Today's drinking water has a slew of contaminants and issues to unravel. Produce used to come hand-picked from a field or tree. Now it is on a grocery store shelf but it is laced with hidden pesticides and genetic manipulations. Genetically modified organisms are then fed to livestock. The days of freshly caught game roasting over a fire are largely impractical now, and this loss shows up as nominal economic growth. At upper Maslow levels, the complexity continues as paper and quill have been replaced by typewriter and then complex computer software programs. The average modern citizen now spends more time learning computer software than the entire organized education experience of people in the 1700's.

Globalism imparts complexity in our life as well. Produce is rarely locally produced but now usually comes from some remote corner of the world. It is now shipped via truck, ship or plane via a complex distribution system and accomplished through complex international treaties and monetary systems.

Complex systems are not necessarily bad, if they work. Modern man has access to fruits and vegetables year round which would be a dream to those of previous societies. But the human mind can only process so much theory and data. The process of idolatry needs to be kept in check by scrutiny that represents a feedback loop. Claims that a commercial product creates love and belonging or esteem need social interaction. This social interaction is a source of complexity as well. But resources for processing this complexity are limited. Unlike other forms of economic deviation, idolatry does not destroy feedback systems, but it does create burdens on them. Complexity increases this burden more and so idolatries flourish and nominal economic status deviates from actual economic status. Complexity does not lead to confusion as much as it leads to a zombie like overloading of the intellect, the weakened state of modern man. The emotion of modern life, which is often created by the media, can also overwhelm the modern intellect.

The new media are one of the strongest feedback loops that exist in modern society. They convey emotional impacts quickly and can reduce the burden of feedback on people through this speed. But they often require substantial financial investment which can increase their representative nature. The feedback that results from their creation can be scarce and far away in time. The invention of new media including print, photography, radio, film television and the internet allows for mass production of images which have strong emotional impacts. The power to represent emotion is not necessarily a bad thing. Life is a journey of emotions and the ability to convey the emotional impact of life's essential moments, even sex and violence, has teaching ability which other ages lacked. But this power also gives us the ability to make powerful idols which confuse us.

Besides emotions, the new media also convey huge amounts of data which potentially help immensely with feedback. Though the amount of information can be overwhelming, without this data, many errors would go unchecked. Consider the amount of health data that is available. Sure, much of it is contradictory and superfluous. But it is a necessary counter measure to the amount of new foods, pollutants and medicines which we have created.

One of the greatest losses in the modern age of media and data is the loss of simple introspection. We have created a world where every problem can be solved by consuming another product from the external world. Meanwhile, we have often ignored the riches of the internal world. Seven billion people exist in this world and all of them have a voice that should be heard, if possible. But the most important voice to the individual remains the voice of the individual himself. Yet the inner voice is often hard to hear amongst the chatter.

It is important to realize that the above discussion deals with the effects on idolatry of honest representativeness only. Representation is when all parties involved are searching for and conveying truth to the best of their ability. Even when this is the case, idolatry can still result in an economy due to feedback issues. However, misrepresentation, the act of deceit, also occurs.

Summary of Idolatry

Idolatry is an inescapable result of human interaction. Nominal values diverge from actual values as a result of distinctiveness, perceived lasting scarcity or abundance and representativeness. Certain aspects of modern life are making idolatry more of a problem such as progress up Maslow's hierarchy, complexity and the representativeness of the media.

But while idolatry is certain to occur, it can overvalue or undervalue a product with the result that elsewhere in society other products' value will change in a balancing fashion. Idolatry does not damage feedback loops, it places burdens on them which overwhelm them. An idol creates an unrealistic value for one item, which is then balanced by changes in the value of other items in the economy.

MATHEMATICAL ECONOMIC EXPRESSION FOR IDOLATRY

As an aside I am including a formula to describe idolatrous phenomenon mathematically. Though the data to use this model may never be practical to attain, a formula will describe idolatry logically and I hope will help differentiate it from other forms of deviation. I have classified idolatry as a form of deviation. Both idolatry and deviation are certain to occur. But they are quite different logically.

Idolatry may be expressed as:
(1) $Id\ v_0 V_0 + Idv_1 V_1 + Idv_2 V_2 + \ldots + Idv_N V_N = $ A Constant
(2) $\Delta V = Idv * V$
(3) $D = V + \Delta V$

where a series or set of relevant items (N) have their demand changes (ΔV) created from and idolatry ratio (Idv) and the value(V) as in Equation (1). The value changes at each point of the demand line in a supply demand curve. The change in value (ΔV) for each item is the product of the idolatry ratio (Idv) and the value (V) as in Equation 2. The demand (D) of a classical supply versus demand curves is the sum of the value

(V) and the change of value (ΔV), either positive or negative. Likewise, idolatry can change the supply curve in a similar fashion as shown in Equation 4 where:

(4) S = W +ΔW = W + Idw *W

S is supply and W is worthiness. As suppliers too fall under different idolatrous beliefs with different idolatry ratios (Idw) the supply curve may change.

If demand side idolatry forces from celebrity endorsement of a chocolate bar increased the value by 50% the idolatry ratio (Id) would be 0.5. Value in this case could mean revenue of both price and quantity. If the market for chocolate bars is fixed and there are ten competing brands losing 5 % each, the idolatry factor for all these brands would be -.05 and the sum would be zero as in equation 1.

(5) 0.50 − .05 -.05 -.05 -.05 -.05 -.05-.05-.05-.05-.05 = 0

Of course, not all change in an item's value are from idolatry.

A creative new candy bar recipe could increase the candy bar market size. This equation is meant as a model to diagnose situations of idolatry.

An example of supply side idolatry might be that a forecaster predicts the price of physical copper will skyrocket in two years so investment funds go to opening copper mines rather than to developing other commodities. The forecast exaggerates the worthiness of copper.

Deviation from Externalities

Deviation from externalities are also certain to occur, but they are more predictable in that, by definition, they occur in one direction since they are not a product of communication error. They form an inversion. In a normal economic situation, the nominal value of a related set of good varies directly with the actual value. When the actual value goes up, the nominal value goes up. The two may not match directly. The actual value might increase twenty percent and the nominal value may only go up fifteen percent. We say that they are directly proportional as in the equation (6) below:

(6) $V_{NOMINAL} \; \alpha \; V_{ACTUAL}$

However, when economic deviation occurs and the nominal measurement employs diminishing returns, nominal and actual economic value are inversely related. When the actual value of a set of goods goes down the nominal value of this same set of goods goes up as in Equation (7) below:

(7) $V_{NOMINAL} \; \alpha \; 1 / V_{ACTUAL}$ (Diminishing Returns)

In the fishing example, the group of items in the sample set would include fish, hooks, nets, boats, gasoline, port real estate, labour and ocean navigation systems, etc. When deviation occurs, as the fish stocks decline the actual value of these commodities decreases but the nominal value increases. The decline in actual value is seen as an increase in nominal value and instead of putting brakes on the situation people are liable to speed it up.

The inversion can also be expressed where the increase in nominal value is an increase in the magnitude of the actual value, but with a negative sign attached.

(8) $V_{NOMINAL} \; \alpha \; V_{ACTUAL} \times (-1)$ (Dichotomous Thinking)

In many ways, dichotomous thinking is the way people naturally evaluate things: they divide items into pleasures which are positive and pains which are negative. When an inversion combines with dichotomous thinking, what is an actual pain will be mentally recorded as a nominal pleasure and vice versa. This is further described in "The Psychology of Economic Actualism".

Do not worry, if you can not understand the formulaic expression as this book is primarily a verbal treatment.

Externalities are a common studied set of economic phenomenon. An externality is a product of an economy which is external to the economy's monetary measurement. Pollution is the most commonly studied example. The smoke being emitted from a smokestack is thought to "hurt" the economy. Conventional economics has long recognized that economic externalities can be damaging but it views this damage as "external" to the economy.

However, conventional economics does not account for the fact that this external damage can actually show up as nominal growth. Deviation from externalities is the process where actual economic impoverishment is nominal wealth creation. Idolatry is the creation of nominal wealth of one item at the expense of the nominal wealth of another item. But deviation from externalities is different in that, while the actual wealth of all declines, the nominal wealth of all, or just an elite few, can increase. The process can go the other way in that an increase in the actual wealth from externalities results in a decline in nominal wealth.

This book will identify five classes of externalities: environmental, leisure, spiritual, error and prevention of damage.

ENVIRONMENTAL EXTERNALITIES

Damage to the environment is, in many ways, a result of many other forms of deviation including dependence on centralization and error such as prevention of damage. These all correlate with environmental damage even if the causational relationship is debatable. Much of the media has spent a great deal of energy describing the negative effects of pollution.

Environmental damage has two main elements to human society, effects upon human health and the loss of natural resources. We do not need to study the magnitude of these effects with economic actualism. This has already been done by others, though more work is needed. But we do need to study how these actual losses can be recorded as nominal gains. To ignore this would be perilous.

Early economic theory placed emphasis on man's society dominating and exploiting natural resources to provide for the basic health of a growing population, and for good reason. Early mankind's life was a constant struggle to socialize and stay alive. Unlike other animals, human beings seem extremely dependent upon society for their survival. After a nine month gestation, the human child takes sixteen or twenty one years to physically mature, and the mental abilities so critical to Man's survival often peak much later. The occasional opportunity to catch fish or pick fruit with our bare hands may be romantic, but we need more than that.

Unlike other animals, every day to survive we need to chop down trees and set fire to them. Without the discovery of fossil fuels, our society would, in its present rate of energy consumption, probably deforest the entire planet in several months. Even if we burnt wood at perfect efficiency, the 8000 Mtoe (million tonnes of oil equivalent) of global energy consumption per year would consume the 283 Gigatons of carbon in global land biomass in 23.4 years. But if efficiencies fell to a more likely 10 percent, we would consume every speck of biomass in two years. While today such a calculation may seem reasonable it would have been unimaginable 500 years ago. The fact that this burning of fuel has grown exponentially throughout human history is disguised by the use of fossil fuels. Even in warmer climates, where heat is not necessary, food must be cooked over fires to prevent food poisoning. We seem built to consume this planet, like it was in our DNA. Environmental degradation seems an inescapable by-product of our society. This consumption of the planet makes us all poorer, though many of us assess the wealth of a society mainly by how much oil it burns.

Western society takes pride in its medical sciences as an example of how we have succeeded in using science to morally conquer adversity from nature. In some ways we have the most advanced medical technology in the world. Using medical imaging we can peer inside the body. We can sequence both our species' and an individual's DNA. We can transplant organs. We are even beginning to grow them in laboratories for transplant purposes, rather than requiring donors. As shown in Figure 14, in North America, we have extended the life expectancy to about 80 from 70 in 1960. This trend roughly extends back to 1900 with a short dip at the end of World War 1. In ancient Europe life expectancy was about 30. Figure 15 shows that the US has decreased infant mortality from about 120 per 1000 live births in 1900 to about 4 in 2000 in New York City, though the rest of the United States and the rest of the developed word show similar statistics.

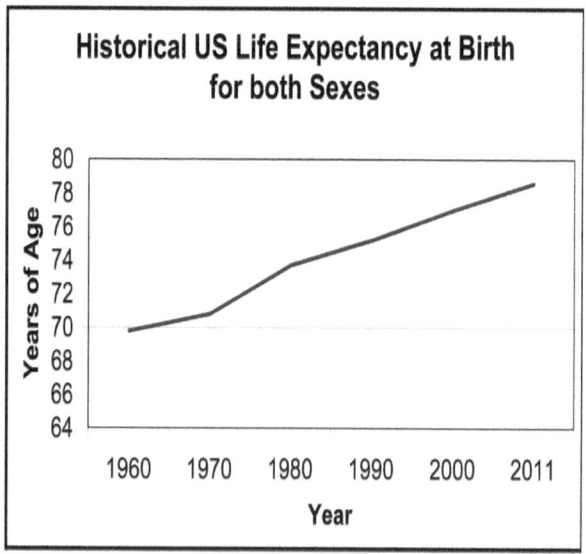

Figure 14 Life expectancy at birth has been rising about one year every five years in the United States recently. Adapted from CDC National Vital Statistics Reports.

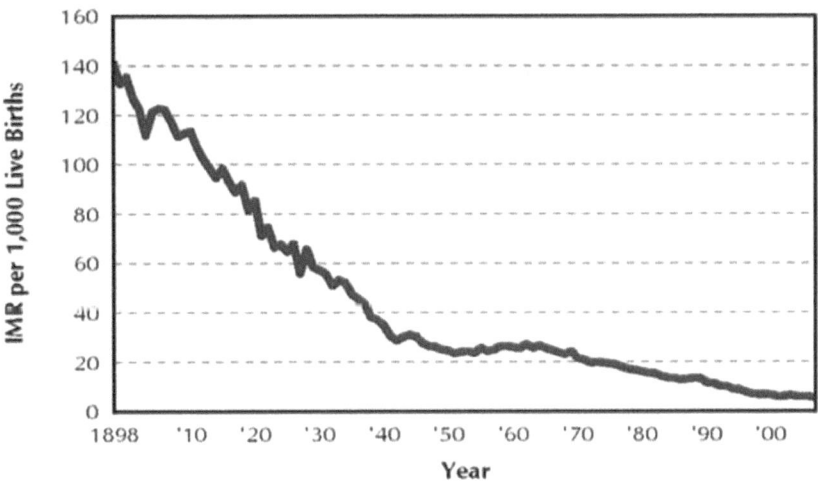

Figure 15 Infant mortality in New York City since 1898 has dropped steadily. The infant mortality in 1898 was probably higher than recorded due to statistical practices. Source: NYC Department of Health & Mental Hygiene. Summary of Vital Statistics (2008)

In 2014, the health care industry is, with education, one of the few remaining economic sectors which is growing. But while life is priceless, health care is not cheap. Paying these expenses can be stressful and that stress is poor for our health. Modern life has many stresses, but when health care now accounts for $211 billion and 11.2 % of the Gross National Product, the effect of this expense on our health should not be ignored. Health care expenses can be a source of stress, which leads to more health care needs and more stress etc., in a spiral that ends in death and financial ruin. We all die eventually. Health care can not change that. But we do not all need to live lives of stress and poverty.

While people had a need for health care before it became expensive, we must account for the fact that some of the need for health care is inadvertently caused by the actual health care industry itself. Health care seems particularly prone to this recursive action. While the effect of mechanics getting in accidents on the way to work may have a miniscule effect on the rate of car accidents, the effect of health care inadvertently skewing health care statistics and causing a need for health care is significant.

It can be argued that the greater the number of abortions, the lower the infant mortality. Aborted babies are often those with less dedicated or wealthy parents. These are the babies that have the highest mortality rate. North America's infant mortality rate has fallen from 120 per 1000 in 1900 to about 4 in 2010 while the abortion rate has risen from very few abortions in 1900, it was illegal so there are poor statistics, to 359 abortions per 1000 live births in 1980 to 228 abortions per 1000 live births in 2010.

Contraception has also reduced the number of unwanted children. But aborting fetuses eight months into term is in the eyes of many, another form of infant mortality that does not show up in infant mortality statistics. This can be described as a form of economic deviation since a decrease in the actual proportion of conceived children that survives pregnancy shows up as an increase in the nominal proportion of conceived children that makes it to three years of age.

In a sense, this inversion is part of an "economic bubble" since it devalues human life in an artificial way. Yet it results in nominal records of improved health. While we may use the term "economic bubble" as a label for historical events like the Tulip Craze or the New Orleans Gold rush, present abortion rates are a new brand of economic horror.

Yet history is likely to view the present abortion inversion as a terrible tragedy, which while it did not provide the media imagery and dramatic narratives of events like mass starvations or the Second World War, still ruined many lives and caused long lasting social damage.

Life expectancy is a statistic that is highly influenced by infant mortality and contraception. The raising of life expectancy is one of the triumphs of both modern medicine and western society in general. Figure 16 shows the trend in life expectancy statistics in the United States since 1930 compared to US life expectancy at birth and conception with the trend in abortion. If we count life expectancy from the time of conception, rather than the moment of birth, the life expectancy curve looks more like the middle curve. While data on abortion rates before it was legalized in 1970 are not available, the graphs show that our medical sciences' and lifestyle improvements' positive effect on life expectancy is debatable.

The life expectancy from the moment of conception may actually be in decline. If we include hypothetical actions from oral contraception like the morning after pill, the life expectancy curve after conception may be even lower. There is probably no accounting for the effects of other means of contraception. Current intercourse rates with pre-World War two methods of contraception would probably result in abysmal life expectancy rates but without modern contraception, modern intercourse rates would be impractical.

So why should we care about life expectancy statistics? Because, most people believe that modern medicine and modern society is creating a healthy society. It is true we have basically conquered many infectious diseases, though newly mutated strains are threatening this progress. But the effect of abortion statistics on life expectancy statistics are covering up some other factor which is lowering the health of the modern citizen.

Environmental hazards, stress and lessening of the quality of the food supply are likely causes. Many other projects have detailed the effects of lessening food quality and environmental hazards upon our health. The point here is that if we look at a set of goods related to our life span and quality of life and include health factors like the war against infectious disease, contraception and life span, a deviation seems to occur. The more money we spend on the set of modern health sciences including modern diets, the lower our life expectancy from conception. But we only see the life expectancy statistic after birth and so we continue in our modern health science direction without caution. Our failure to check for deviation leads us to mismanage our health care and lifestyle consumption set.

A similar deviation occurs with the creation of pharmaceutical drugs. The first synthetic drug, chloral hydrate, was discovered in 1869. In 2014 there were approximately 87,000 drugs listed on the National Drug Code of the FDA. While many of these are dosage variations, the number of drugs has become enormous. Synthetic psychoactive drugs are recently increasing rapidly from being uninvented to about 350 which people are known to take recreationally. The massive increase in the consumption of pharmaceuticals pollutes the environment as unused medications and the metabolic wastes from used medications are discharged into the environment. We in turn, ingest trace amounts of numerous pharmaceuticals in our drinking water. The effects of most of these numerous contaminants are largely unknown, perhaps since the explosion in the use of pharmaceuticals has been so recent. But the effects

Introducing Economic Actualism

year	# of Abortions	# Abortions per 100 births	# Births/ (#Births plus Abortions)	Life Expectancy at Birth	Life Expectancy at Conception
1930		0.007	0.99993	59.7	59.695821
1935		0.007	0.99993	61.7	61.695681
1940		0.007	0.99993	62.9	62.895597
1940		0.007	0.99993	62.9	62.895597
1950		0.007	0.99993	68.2	68.195226
1950		0.007	0.99993	68.2	68.195226
1960	292	0.007	0.99993	69.7	69.695121
1965	794	0.021	0.99979	69.7	69.685363
1970	193491	5.19	0.9481	70.8	67.12548
1975	1034200	32.89	0.6711	72.6	48.72186
1980	1553890	39	0.5698	73.7	41.99426
1985	1588550	39	0.5776	74.7	43.14672
1990	1608620	38.68	0.6132	75.4	46.23528
1995	1359440	34.86	0.6514	75.8	49.37612
2000	1312990	32.35	0.6765	77	52.0905
2005	1206200	29.15	0.7085	77.8	55.1213
2010	1102700	27.57	0.7243	78.7	57.00241

Abortions and effect on Life Expectancy in the United States from 1930-2010

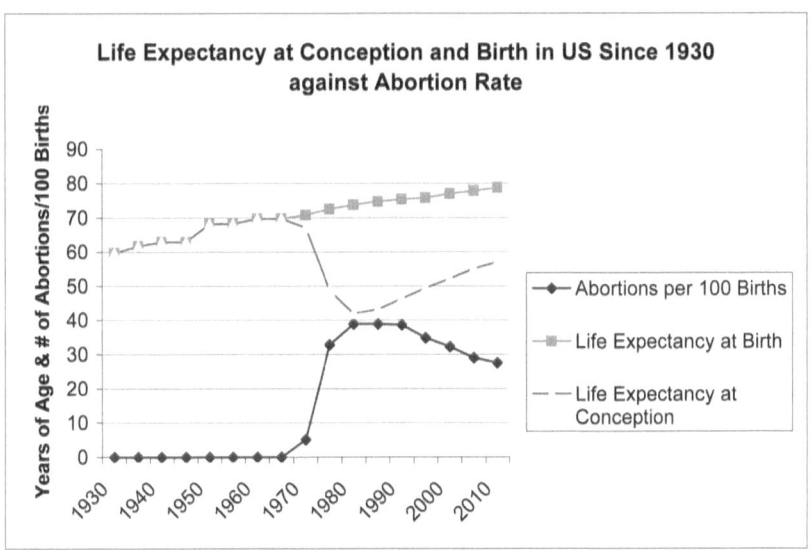

Figure 16 United States Life Expectancy at Birth and Life Expectancy at Conception against Abortion from 1930 to 2010.

of some other chemicals in the environment, such as the use of pesticides, have been shown to be dramatic. Pesticides are often endocrine disruptors, which like some pharmaceuticals, can interfere with the hormonal balances of the body to the extent that affected wildlife such as fish or amphibians can grow sex organs from both genders. While human biology has more defences against these and other effects, we are not immune. The increased use of biological chemistry can create disease. This sounds trite, but it is a form of economic deviation this is usually perilously ignored.

Just as lessening of health can be seen as economic growth in health services, so too, damage to the environment can show up as economic growth. We saw the fishery used as an example of this earlier; how a fish caught with the bare hands or a wooden stick produces the same good but with not nearly as much nominal wealth as a modern trawler roaming the high seas for global markets.

But many aspects of our modern society which we celebrate as economic growth, are really cases of environmental damage. When we focus our attention on the nominal record of a situation, and many of us do when we look at things like financial statements, we can lose sight of the actual. The actual situation and its nominal record often differ. When the nominal record increases due to a decline in the actual situation, an economic deviation occurs. This is certain to occur. So when our society or our environment suffers actual losses we often celebrate, seeing only nominal gain.

Introducing Economic Actualism

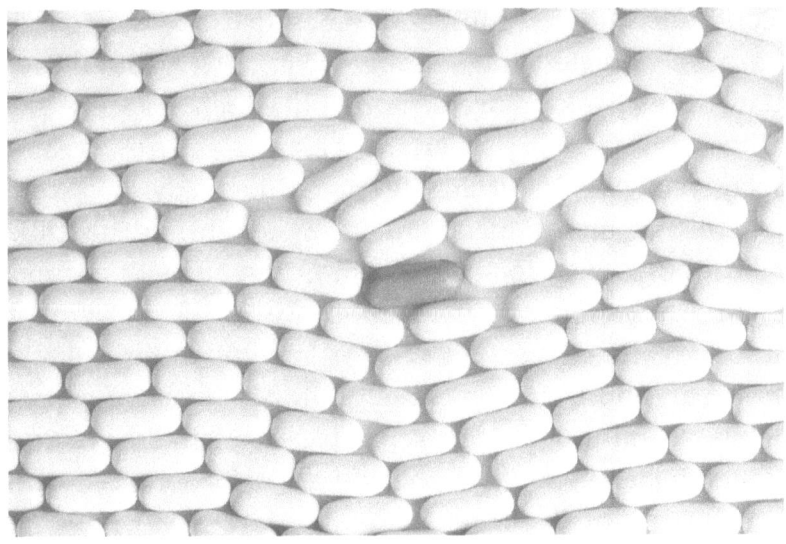

© Serrnovik – Dreamstime.com

Figure 17 In 2014, the US National Drug Code listed 87,000 drugs of which you may need only one.

To some extent, environmental damage motivates economic growth. The deforestation of Europe motivated the coal industry which motivated the industrial revolution which motivated the steam engine. Mankind is on a constant treadmill of devising new energy sources and new technologies to replace the one that came before, but which are rendered obsolete due to increasing scarcity on the local scale. When North American petroleum or natural gas is consumed near population centers, transportation systems and pipelines are constructed for importation. And foreign relations may be necessitated. The nominal economic growth usually at least greatly exaggerates the actual improvement. But it is often a deviation.

Until somebody invents a fail-safe fusion reactor that can operate cheaply on a small scale, or taps into the immense potential of solar energy, this nominal growth at the expense of actual growth from the dwindling of resources is certain to continue. Other resources besides fish and energy that have been depleted include: game, lumber, ground water and surface drinking water, top soil which does not need fertilizer, beachfront property, parklands and reserves and reliable weather without climate change. Basically, any worldly resource that men depend upon for health and happiness has been ransacked to some extent in the name of economic growth. And as the nominal economic wealth has grown, our failure to realize the actual loss has sped up cycle after cycle of boom and bust until, eventually, all 7 billion or more of us will be screaming at the seams for space exploration before the entire planet explodes from the poverty of its nominal wealth.

SPIRITUALITY

But man does not live on bread alone. Although most economists tend to ignore this, much of his life is spiritual. Whether you believe in God, atheism, or a mixture of the two, we can all recognize that some people who live in poverty, both actual and nominal, manage to be happy. Yet many wealthy people can be very unhappy. Spirituality, the ability to find joy regardless of circumstances, is perhaps the greatest source of wealth of all for those who learn or are blessed to attain it. Yet spirituality, this greatest source of actual wealth, is often a threat to nominal wealth.

Let us consider the seven deadly sins: wrath, greed, sloth, pride, lust, envy and gluttony as illustrated in Figure 18. Even if you are not a Roman Catholic, this doctrine is an important influence on western culture. Each of these deadly sins make us miserable when they occur, and their occurrence seems to be certain, especially in modern society. Yet while each of them destroys actual wealth with venomous precision, each of them can also be a source of nominal wealth. And as such, the economy applauds their increase.

Introducing Economic Actualism

© Ryan Deberardinis – Dreamstime

Figure 18 The seven deadly sins are always trying to tell us where to go.

Wrath destroys lives and creates wars. It leads to conflict which we will discuss later but wrath causes people to buy weapons, to fight wars and to incur injuries upon each other which require medical services. Yet while outright war may allow wrath to be let loose and even celebrated, even in peacetime wrath can be a powerful economic stimulus and motivator of behaviour. The hidden wounds in all of our hearts will, when given an attitude of unforgiven revenge, turn even the most civil behaviour with an inner meanness that can drive economic actors like a whip cracking a horse borne carriage. Often the drive to scale the company ladder is generated by repressed rage, rage that could have been generated from even a minor slight in childhood that was never resolved. It is a barren style of life from an actualist perspective, yet it can create nominal economic growth.

Such wrath motivated behaviour can often display itself as greed, the obsession with increasing nominal wealth when there is no genuine need for it. Greed is the tax man's pot of gold at the end of the rainbow since it is surplus wealth that is easy to siphon.

It is a good question if greed for actualist wealth can even exist. Can we be excessively happy in a genuine sense? Surely, one individual can be excessively joyous if it creates misery for others. But in a free economy with actualist tendencies, the temptation to be happy at the expense of others is minimized. A society can not be said to be excessively joyous if the joy is actual and inclusive, but the nominalist greed of North America in the latter twentieth century can not be said to have caused excess joy. Our greed for nominal wealth often seems to have been at the expense of actual wealth.

Sloth is that deep depression which leaves us slumped on the couch unwilling or unable to care for ourselves, dependent upon the nominal wealth of our society when we would be better off using our free energies in efforts outside of the nominal economy. Sloth is not just a matter of being off the time card at work. Buddhist monks spend immense amounts of time sitting quietly, doing nothing. But they are not indulging in sloth. They are actively meditating. While no government statistic can discern whether someone is meditating or being slothful, the individual can tell.

Just as meditation is a source of actual wealth beyond nominal measurement, so sloth, with its despair boredom and depression, is a state of actual poverty beyond nominal measurement. But slothful people can be a source of economic demand and therefore, nominal economic growth. For the slothful man requires ready made snacks and a television set, plus appliances and servants to do his housework. He may even need pills to elevate his mood.

Pride, the refusal to be humble, can destroy lives while building economic growth. Perhaps the most dangerous type of pride is pride in nominalism. Nominalism can generate extreme self-righteousness, even when it can not be defended or verbally expressed. For nominalists follow the rules and perform their deeds, both good and bad, in the cause which they believe is the greatest show on earth, or at least the practical vicinity. Often the more illiterate people are, the least able to express themselves, the more proud they are to cling to their nominalist cause, whatever cause that may be. Pride can become a source of meaning in life, but when misguided this meaning can ruin lives while creating an illusion of nominal prosperity. Yet pride in nominalism is encouraged in many ways. Nominalists can be very proud people and we are all partly nominalists.

Lust is an intense overwhelming desire, not necessarily for sex, but for anything. Such uncontrollable lust is created by idolatry, the imbibing of social value to something it does not deserve. Yet our economy grows from the creation of such desires. Sexual lust can fuel fashion, cosmetics, culture, even housing and cars. Lust for status can fuel the demand for these same items. It can be argued that, since the business model for much of our media revolves around being paid for providing a platform for lust creation either in magazines, newspaper, TV or radio, that even when our culture achieves higher levels it is really only preparing us for lust. Lust fuels the fires of our nominal growth while worsening our actual decay.

Envy is the opiate of fools. The true quality of our lives is best left to be judged by God, or professionals when worldly needs require judgment. But when we self-righteously judge our lives with those of others, looking for things to complain about and feel self-righteous, we get caught in a never ending spiral of consumption. No matter what our circumstance, we can always envy others. When we are poor we can envy the rich, imagining their life of ease and simplicity. Yet many a rich man has envied the uncomplicated life of a peasant. For beyond a certain level of income, money does not raise self-evaluations of happiness very much at all. Envy keeps you constantly trying to cross the fence to get to the greener side, no matter which side you are on. It generates nominal activity and actual misery. Yet the process of economic salesmanship constantly promotes envy. Envy creates the economic demand which causes nominal growth but perpetuates unhappiness.

Gluttony can be more than just eating too much. It can be obsessing over the quality of food or other products you consume. Often these obsessions are over the idol of the current trend. But gluttony of any type leads to actual unhappiness. Gluttony of food can lead to health problems. It can also lead to harmful social practices such as the force feeding of ducks to make their livers large and other animal cruelties. But gluttony of other products can lead to slave labour as well, often in the pursuit of false idols which would be abandoned if the true costs of their practices were paid.

In contrast to the seven deadly sins are the seven heavenly virtues: patience, charity, diligence, humility, chastity, kindness and temperance. These are qualities which improve the actual wealth of the individual and the society but often detract from the nominal wealth. The kingdom of God is within you (Luke 17:21).

Yet despite the efforts of numerous religious leaders, the seven deadly sins seem an inevitable product of human society. The thoughts of Man are continually upon evil (Genesis 6:5). The mindless ants may labour in perfect civility in their respective prosperous kingdoms, but mankind is plagued by wrath, greed, sloth, pride, lust envy and gluttony. These spirits rob us of our actual wealth while promoting nominal wealth. While the devil may exist, he does not seem to require a visual presence for these spirits to do their works. Mankind embraces them naturally.

Freudians often say that people have limited resistance to sales techniques. They can only say "No" so many times before their psychological "No" muscles get tired and they give in to say "Yes". In many ways our modern culture is an anti-culture in that it does not provide a culture of health but provides a culture where we must constantly say "no" to the seven deadly sins until eventually we get tired, say "yes", and get out our credit card or stuff our head in the fridge or some other bad surrender to nominalist forces which may take the form of one of the seven deadly sins, or maybe a novel sin of our own device and demise. Whether it be semi-pornographic magazine covers in the grocery story that belittle our defences or a news broadcast that gets under our skin, or a coveted object in our neighbour's possession, it all wears us down. These things belittle our actual wealth and happiness while creating nominal wealth.

And they are inescapable. The effects may not be directly recorded monetarily, but their effects upon nominal activity are inescapable. Patience is turned into wrath by a hectic life style, where everything is "go, go, go" and everyone must exist within an economic cubby hole where their only allowable contribution is to be a cog in the machine. Charity is turned to greed through a spirit of cynicism and self-pity. Diligence is turned to sloth when the tasks before us seem overwhelming, even in a modern society of instant appliances. Humility is turned to pride as we embark on economic trades up the Maslow pyramid. We are proud to purchase our self-actualization. Chastity towards creating actual wealth in our own life and those of others is turned to lust due to pervasive and powerful media and sales techniques. Kindness turns to envy due to our sufferings for the nominalist causes and our belief that others benefit when in fact, everyone loses. And temperance turns to gluttony as consumption is touted as the cure to economic ills. This is a cursory glance at the process by which the seven heavenly virtues are converted into the seven deadly sins in the name of nominal economic growth. It is a subject for the centuries.

Throughout history, society has been a constant struggle of the confusion between nominal and actual status. While spirituality is impossible to record numerically, it is a major and perhaps the essential battlefield.

LEISURE

Leisure, the time available to do what you want after you do what is required, is a friend of actualism and an adversary of nominalism. Leisure is a source of actual wealth. It allows social discussion and political debate. It allows for the prevention of disease through rest and exercise. It allows for amusement and artistry which often expresses the hidden underlying problems of the society. It leads to a more stable society by preventing the hazards of the business cycle from becoming too extreme. To many, particularly the young, leisure is really the purpose of life, a reason to endure the nominal requirements of society.

© Wakebreakmedia Ltd – Dreamstime.com

Figure 19 Leisure can be a source of actual wealth in many ways such as maintenance of health and happiness while spurring economic demand. Yet, in some means of accounting, leisure only decreases nominal wealth.

Yet for nominalists, and we are all partly nominalists, leisure is the enemy. Leisure lets people to their own devices when they should be working to pay more taxes. Leisure allows people to discuss matters which those in charge find to be difficult or embarrassing. While many nominalist systems are riddled with crime that is justified as "legal" by the powers that be, leisure time allows people to create mischief of their own device. People with leisure time, when it is improperly spent, get drunk or smoke pot or gamble without government sanction or tell bad jokes or any number of things that are regarded as imprudent.

Just as behaviours taking place within a building of government are not automatically actions of governance, and behaviours taking place in industry are not automatically productive, proper or profitable, so too, time spent in leisure is not automatically fun, productive or conducive to liberty.

Government and industry go to extensive lengths to ensure that activities within their domain are suitable. Employees must be trained, instructed and scrutinized and control measures are put in place. Yet errors still occur despite this effort. So, too, every man when left to his own leisure must not collapse into self-indulgence.

We must actively plan leisure with the same dedication we do to our work. We have as much duty to our leisure as we do to our industrial and government duties. In fact, our duty to leisure may be greater as we do not have the nominalist style of excuses, "I was just following orders" that we do in work and government.

Perhaps one of the saddest aspects of modern society is how the increase in unemployment and leisure time has failed to be matched by an increase in the ability to use it. Proper use of leisure requires independence, morality and discernment. Of the three, working on a punch clock often requires only morality. Independence and discernment are not essential when you are taking orders. Yet they are essential when you are planning leisure if you want it to lead to happiness, independence and prosperity.

A teenager who spends her spare money on an expensive rock concert because she "has to go" when it will only promote corporate sloganeering, illicit drugs and unwise sex may not be proper leisure at all. Doing something because "everyone else is" with your spare time can acquaint you with the current trend, but it may not serve you as an individual. Discerning what will serve you with your spare time is a key to actual wealth.

Consider meditation. Meditation can seem like the ultimate in doing nothing, yet it can also be considered the most essential form of work. For while meditation looks like sloth, it is actually the greatest diligence: an inspection of your own thoughts and feelings. Nothing could require less financial investment and yet be more crucial. But you do not need to follow nominal dictates and travel thousands of miles to a special temple and sit in an awkward posture to meditate. It helps, but you can also meditate while waiting for the bus if you practice. The quality of our inner thoughts escapes nominal measurement. But unless we have some leisure time to compose and reflect, this most crucial aspect of our lives will suffer actual neglect.

While properly spent leisure time can spur new markets in fields like entertainment, travel and education, most economists tend to neglect this benefit. The mantra instead is "full employment" and "job creation" as if only productive activity can occur within the confines of a punch card. It does not matter if these "jobs" do not provide a living wage. Such a slight would seem innocent except that most economists derive their income from an interest rate on the debts which are created, rather than for producing actual benefit, so having immense numbers of people trapped in long hours of unproductive work and going into debt is regarded as "wealth creation". The wealth created from such a situation is nominal, not actual.

A lack of leisure time helps ensure the preservation of the present business cycle, enhancing its nominal wealth. Without leisure to explore other economic possibilities, the present business cycle can be maintained, but to an unstable level. Its nominal data can deviate excessively from actual reality so that when the business cycle must change, and all business cycles do, its change is cataclysmic.

Leisure is an externality in that, while its costs and benefits are real, they lie largely outside of nominal economic measurement. Leisure is an actual wealth that is recorded as a nominal loss of income. Yet as leisure increases actual wealth, it also increases effectiveness. The free time allows us to examine and improve the assumptions of the business cycle through better negotiation.

ERROR

Error is an obvious source of actual loss. Yet it can also be a source of nominal gain. Sometimes, the pursuit of error for nominal gain is intentional. A manufacturing attitude of designed obsolescence keeps consumers replacing goods. Nominally, this shows as new goods being consumed constantly when they are actually more goods of lesser value. Our education system now gives degrees at exorbitant costs that are out of date within a few years of graduation. So while nominally, we are more educated the marginal value of this education seems to be less and less, though we pay more and more for it. Error is an ever present a source of inversion on the macroeconomic scale.

On the microeconomic scale, error is only an inversion when the market is captive, when there is no meaningful competition and where the producer has a monopoly. Otherwise, the error will result in the repeat sale to the producer's competition. But our economy has largely moved away from lassie faire competition towards state controlled monopolies, trade union monopolies and corporate oligarchies. The consumer has been the victim as vast amounts of nominal consumption are producing successively smaller amounts of satisfaction.

PREVENTION OF LOSS

A specific type of error that creates an inversion is prevention of loss. Buying a fire extinguisher is a minor actual purchase but it can prevent loss of an entire home. Without this purchase, the insurance company may provide an entire new house, a great nominal expense but actually not much different than the one gutted by flames. Construction made to proper standards can also prevent the necessary inversion of building replacement.

But health care is probably the best example where prevention of loss can form an inversion. Going to the minor expense of a healthier diet and suitable exercise can prevent the inversion of major surgeries with their exorbitant costs. Modern North America is being consumed by the high cost of our advanced health care for emergency intervention and our relatively poor abilities of disease prevention.

INEFFECTIVENESS

Effectiveness is the ability to do the right thing; the right choice among numerous alternatives. The loss of effectiveness is another inevitable aspect of economic activity. In addition to certain economic inversion, where actual wealth is nominal poverty and vice versa, an economy is certain to develop problems with the loss of effectiveness. This contrasts with another economic concept of efficiency. Efficiency is the ability to do something well, even if it is a bad choice.

Ineffectiveness is different than inversion. Inversion is a mathematical relationship where:

$$V_{ACTUAL} \alpha\ 1/\ V_{NOMINAL}$$

The loss of effectiveness is a lack of choice, either generally or in a biased direction. A loss of effectiveness in a biased direction is where for some reason an economic choice is unavailable, such as a certain style of clothing, but it is recognized as a loss of choice, not seen as an increase of value as in an inversion.

However, when ineffectiveness combines with an inversion, when alternative choices are lost and the resulting actual loss from this choice is only seen as a nominal gain, the results are both devastating and dramatic. A "bubble" forms. Even if participants recognize this bubble is forming they may unable to escape its formation as duress compels them to participate. They may require one crucial product from the economy such as housing or food and are thus unable to stop participating in a whole slew of other economic transactions.

A bubble seems like a very harmless term but the social outcomes can be horrific. The term "bubble" gives the impression that no damage is created once it bursts. But economic bubbles can ruin lives, destroy environments, precipitate wars and crumble societies. "Cancerous instability" may be more suitable as it conveys the potential ugliness of the phenomena, though it is not used in the common vernacular.

FINANCIAL OBLIGATIONS

Previous financial arrangements inevitably reduce our effectiveness in choosing future financial arrangements. This is true for both the consumer and the producer. This may seem like a foreign concept to some in the climate of unlimited credit of twenty first century America, but it is a truism. Twenty-first century America is largely run with fiat currency, money which is not only a fiat paper currency representation of wealth but an electronic representation of this paper. It creates a lack of choice for the borrower as they are obligated to pay but creates no ineffectiveness for the primary lender since it is generated by a computer with infinite money creation potential.

Ineffectiveness of the borrower is caused by financial obligations. Costs of living which are mandated by the economy also cause ineffectiveness. For the consumer, "discretionary income" is the money left over for free spending after the essentials of life and financial commitments are taken care of. For producers, fixed costs such as overhead can reduce their discretionary investments. Producers often use the term "liquidity" to describe the assets they have available for economic decisions.

Non-discretionary spending is a trapped, static, base of behaviour and is a source of ineffectiveness. It locks us into previously made decisions. Ineffectiveness can bias our future decision making, until a choice is no longer available. Many consider Beta to have been a technically superior video tape than VHS yet, like two snow balls going down a hill, VHS grew faster and eventually gained a monopoly. Many fashion styles are not readily available on the present market because the mass production fashion industry has not financially committed themselves to that style at the present time. The financial ability to provide these lost alternates was lost.

The loss of effectiveness can effect both borrower and lender. The borrower is trapped into making regular payments and the lender is prevented from using his financial resources for other means. Some examples of losses of effectiveness due to previous financial decisions like fashion are not terribly important. But often effectiveness can be lost with more important matters such as when the position of roads and infrastructure and the culture of home construction mandates subdivision construction on prime agricultural lands. Medicines often are subject to loss of effectiveness. While Aspirin is often touted as a miracle drug since it can cure everything from joint pain to blood thinning to heart attack prevention, if it was discovered recently it would probably be banned since it has side effects of thinning the lining of the stomach.

When money was backed by real resources such as gold, there was a limited amount of money which could be lent into the system. But this assumption is gradually eroding in modern western society. Under a system called "fractional reserve banking", American banks were gradually allowed to lend out more money than they had as assets, the fraction going as low as one dollar of cash reserves for every twenty dollars which were lent. The United States Federal Reserve, the private organization that prints money for the Government of the United States of America, has been allowed to lend out money recklessly with few limits. They lend money that does not exist, lessening effectiveness for borrowers without creating obligation for the lender since, for the lender, there is no actual commitment.

These financial obligations are also partly an inversion. The loss of financial freedom shows up on balance sheets as a creation of wealth. Our activities outside of an economy are largely unrecorded but our debts are noted in perpetuity. Some of the most ancient archaeological clay tablets are records of debts from thousands of years ago. The records of our present financial obligations may outlive any of our other accomplishments. But they will be evidence of nominal wealth, even if their main result was our lack of effective choice regarding future decisions.

In fact most Americans, and much of the world since US money has been the global reserve currency of the late twentieth century, have no discretionary income. Their income does not cover their living expenses and they must borrow money that does not exist to pay for an economy which offers little choice about many essential aspects of their lives. This combination of inversion and loss of choice is creating a global bubble, or cancerous instability, of uncertain future.

CONFLICT

An act that creates an inversion often is a form of idolatry and often reduces effectiveness as well. While economic behaviour is simplified by monetary prices it always has inherently complex underlying causes and outcomes. Conflict is a form of deviation that can have all of the above effects.

Conflict is an inevitable aspect of life. Though we try, we can not escape it. While military battle may the first thing the word "conflict" brings to mind, conflict comes in an infinite variety of forms: interpersonal, business, inner family, between families, cultural, legal and military, both overt and covert. What we fight for is usually some aspect of idolatry, but it creates inversions and ineffectiveness very quickly and often in a cancerous instability.

© Branex – Dreamstime.com

Figure 20 Conflict can give us nominal wealth but actual poverty. Yet it can also reduce our freedom.

While I have classified conflict in its numerous forms primarily as a source of ineffectiveness, it has a large inversion process as well. A lot of people like to sell bullets. It is one of the few markets where the buyer pursues the seller. The more we collectively spend on conflict, the more we suffer yet the more our nominal wealth increases. Military spending is a prime example. Just as the global fishing industry has astronomically more nominal wealth to catch the same fish as catching fish with the bare hands does, so modern military spending has created a massive industry with little practical benefits. At the height of the cold war, the USA and USSR had enough thermonuclear weapons combined to obliterate the entire population of the globe about 3000 times. This is an astronomical increase in military capacity growing at an exponential rate. Contrast this with traditional martial arts such as karate which, while producing little nominal wealth, is even a source of spiritual strength for many of its proficient practitioners.

The maniacal spread of military arms is a topic that has received coverage over the years, yet it is only one type of conflict. Interpersonal conflict on an emotional level can severely reduce actual wealth yet spawn an industry of self-help books, counsellors and pharmaceuticals. Even real estate purchases are often motivated both by the uncontrolled desires of newlyweds and the inability to live together afterwards with offspring. Interpersonal conflict often overlaps with spiritual health, but the effects on nominal wealth and actual wealth, while inverse, are both enormous.

The growth of the legal industry also increases nominal wealth. While the actual costs of legal conflict may be less than the costs of conflicts carried out by illegal means, the growth of this legal industry is an inversion: its increase in nominal wealth signifies an actual malaise. Both business conflicts and personal conflicts generate this inversion and ineffectiveness.

We conflict over two main categories, resources and idolatries. Yet as we have progressed up the Maslow hierarchy our conflict over resources is increasingly a conflict over idolatries in disguise. Even when we fight over oil, an essential commodity for modern agriculture, we fight over it increasingly because it gives us a lifestyle we consider to be stylish. Even two children fighting over their lunch money are often fighting over their rank in the schoolyard pecking order. Often, our conflicts have increasingly little to do with resources at all. We might fight wars over "democracy" or have family disputes over "fairness". While such causes can be used as reasons to fight over resources, in a world of increasing conflict the fighting over idolatries grows constantly. The pen is mightier than the sword or gun. While ideas can be the ultimate weapons, any power raises the potential for misuse and injury.

Yet, conflict when it arises, can drastically reduce effectiveness. So while it has inversion components I have elected to categorize it primarily as a source of ineffectiveness. Some conflict, such as reasoned discussion which I aim for in this book, is necessary to keep idolatry in line. Yet unresolved conflicts confine our choice. Whether it be in the bedroom or the battlefield, whether covert or overt, the process of fighting can force us to make decisions we instantaneously regret but can never take back. Without forgiveness, fighting restricts what we do, what we can say, where we live, who we can associate with and even what we believe. Conflict is the ultimate restriction on our freedom. When two countries are at war they become committed to the conflict until it is settled, often when one side runs out of ammunition. When a couple divorces, it commits them to take a different look at the relationship forever. A fight on the school yard can commit children into adult attitudes and behaviours they don't even recognize. Only forgiveness can restore effectiveness, and it can only occur once the conflict has run its course or peacekeeping has mitigated the situation.

DEPENDENCE UPON CENTRALIZATION

If it were not for the issue of dependence upon centralization, economic actualism would be much easier to apply. All of the other deviation issues, while inevitable, are one sided. The less environmental damage we have, the better. The more spirituality we have, the better. The more leisure we have, the better. The less error we have, the better. The more prevention and less damage we have, the better. The less conflict, the better. The less financial obligations the better. The less erroneous talk in the form of idolatry, the better. But dependence upon centralization is a little different. For centralization of power, we need the right amount.

Centralization is a social relationship and Man is a social animal. Man has: a biology that requires long standing family rearing in childhood, an adulthood that requires community to survive, and an intellect to know how to misbehave and abuse his society. The issues of man's social involvement is not a one sided outcome. Rare and isolated stories from historical records exist of orphans of unknown origin who are found living outside of society. They usually have no discernable language, excellent olfactory abilities and animal-like running skills, but it does not seem like an enviable life. And these uncivilized orphaned children were suspected to have lived largely by eating society's garbage and sleeping in garages and the like.

Man benefits from having social involvement, yet he is also prone to excessive centralization. This centralization is an inversion as any participation in an economy generates that society's records while it negates the opportunity costs of activity outside of an economy. Centralization also reduces effectiveness as it requires commitment to that society to the exclusion of outside activity. But unlike other forms of inversion and ineffectiveness it has beneficial and necessary outcomes as well.

Determining the proper level of centralization and its aspects is the essential discourse of politics and of history. Without laws and rules, human interaction descends into anarchy. An ant seems to have decent behaviour ingrained into its DNA. We don't. Humans need rules. Yet who polices the policeman? And in our modern society we have many types of policeman: teachers who regulate language, professional associations that regulate their trade, government bureaucrats who regulate general society, corporations that regulate their business offerings and militaries that regulate their border. The list is endless. The pros and cons of social organization have created a debate that has rung through the millennia with sometimes violent results.

Some centralization of social power seems essential in human society, yet it creates both inversions and ineffectiveness and also leads to idolatry. Money creation is perhaps the essential economic inversion. Modern fiat currency is, by itself, totally worthless. Yet as monetization occurs, and as people record more of their resources and time with fiat money, the economy is seen to grow even if this growth is a cancerous instability. Centralization of power increases numerical records of wealth in the eyes of that social power, even if the society is becoming impoverished in actuality.

Centralization of power decreases effectiveness as it places decisions in the hands of people who are both distanced and less interested in the results. Totalitarian societies are notorious for having leaders that once appealed to the masses for their empathy but whose decisions were impractical for their followers later on. But by that time the options for alternatives have been lost due to the dictator's powers. Some historians claim Hitler would have gone down in history as one of the twentieth century's greatest leaders if he had not invaded Poland. Hitler seemed to symbolize their struggles and gained an idolatrous image. He was a master at propaganda, exciting German crowds into irrational expectations. These expectations may have acquired a force he could not stop. The Germans needed to pick their spirits up. They were demoralized after World War One and Hitler empathized with Germany's frustrations with the reparations enforced by the Treaty at Versailles. He unified German peoples who had been scattered into neighbouring countries like Austria, Hitler's place of birth. Certainly Neville Chamberlain, Britain's Prime Minister before World War Two, had high hopes that Hitler could bring Europe back into an equitable situation. Yet somehow, Hitler in his isolated cocoon of idolatry and raging crowds made a decision that was ineffective, that also led to conflict creating inversions, and Germany fell into a cancerous instability that it and the world could not escape, despite almost everyone recognizing that the world was on the wrong path. When we centralize decision making, we risk making those decisions ineffective both from the viewer of the subject of the decision and, ultimately, the maker of the decision as well.

Centralization also creates the risk for idolatry for several reasons. It increases both the need for communication and the remoteness of the communicator from his subject of conversation while it can also interfere with the feedback that helps keep his communication in check. The example of Hitler is one of idolatry as he became an icon for the Nazi party which was infamous for its staged public events and symbols. Yet to those outside of the rallies, Hitler worship was meaningless and dangerous babbling. Hitler's ambitions necessitated his keen interest in all forms of media at the time including, movies, music, parades, symbols, slogans, books, painting and public spectacle. But the communication was primarily in one direction. Hitler's power increasingly isolated him. While this isolation increased his need for feedback from the German people, he didn't get it. "Heil Hitler" had become the opening salutation between military personal. And it was not advisable for an ordinary German citizen to write Adolph Hitler and tell him that his plans were misguided. Hitler died from his ineffectiveness, idolatry and inversion when he committed suicide in a bunker in Berlin just before the end of the war. As is often the case when a "bubble" bursts, the devastation has lasted long after the expansion bursts. The world has never been the same.

The Nazis have become emblematic of the problems of excess power concentration in the twentieth century but numerous other abuses of power have occurred. The technology of the twentieth century has made centralization of power much easier to establish, though apparently not that much easier to exercise appropriately. George Orwell in his 1948 book "1984" wrote a work of science fiction that many regard from the perspective of the twenty first century as being science fact. Yet most of us stay silent in our quiet desperation which is a source of the first principle of economic actualism: uncertainty.

Chapter Three

Uncertainty

While deviations are certain to occur in the form of inversions, idolatry and ineffectiveness, another means by which actual economic reality differs from nominal economic data stems from the process of economic measurement. Economics measures rational behaviour. The more rational behaviour a good or service is imbibed with, the higher its price. The more rational behaviour a person performs in the form of labour, training and wise decisions the more money he earns. The more rational demand there is for a resource and the scarcer its supply, the more money it is worth.

Our economic system has an "invisible hand" which, through the interaction of participants measures the rational worth of goods and services and generates a single value, the price, as an indicator of this measurement. But besides deviation, there is another cost to this measurement. The process of measuring "rationality" alters the nature of rationality. This alteration is uncertain in its direction.

In many ways, this uncertainty caused by economic participation is essential to understanding the human experience. We are all forced by our compulsory social participation to use a set of worthless, or fiat, nominal symbols which acquire a nominal value from the act of our participation: a key element is social feedback. To paraphrase Mr. Spock from the original Star Trek television series "This thing we call language is most remarkable. We all depend upon it for so very much, but is any of us really its master?"

The philosopher Heidegger concurred when he said "Man acts as though he were the shaper and master of language, while in fact language remains the master of man. " Language is just one aspect of the nominal symbols which make up a society. None of us can claim to have a monopolistic control on the creation of nominal economic status. This economic uncertainty is an inescapable aspect of human life, though its psychological implications and its management is discussed further in "The Psychology of Economic Actualism".

Economic interaction, in both free societies and dictatorships, is the bond that holds a civilization together. Man is a communal animal. He gathers in sets of behaviours called economies. Just as flocks of birds or schools of fish can move with beautiful, even mesmerizing, choreographies which pulse back and forth or circle in tornado like swirls without displaying an indisputable leader, so economies can pulse, not with physical position and movement, but with ideological assessment of rationality. Yet just as a flock of birds or a school of fish can move to the left or right, seemingly at random, so a society can change its ideological beliefs back and forth, even without centralized decision makers, though modern social elites have unprecedented power to orchestrate the process of oscillation. But while animals indicate their flocking with physical positioning, a society's ideological herding has two indicators: price and culture. Price is the dominant indicator while culture acts primarily as a feedback mechanism to correct deviations and uncertainties regarding prices.

This feedback is an essential social component for, without feedback, all manners of insanities may be transformed into enforced rationalities. An economy without feedback can quickly turn into a disaster with long lasting consequences. The act of measuring a good or service by the assumptions of the economy's present business cycle will change that good's or service's value. It has one value outside of measurement and another after measurement which is symbolized by a price.

Consider the spare time of a young adult on the weekend, say five hours on a Saturday afternoon. This is free time and the person can use

© Chris Van Lennep – Dreamstime.com

Figure 21 Birds of many feathers flock together.

it at their discretion either within the local economy or outside of economic participation. This time has an inherent value even if it is not used for participation in the local economy. It can be used for study, religion, courtship, exercise, cooking, home improvement and housekeeping, socializing, volunteer work or all manner of activities that generate actual wealth but do not generate nominal wealth and may be a nominal expense. These possible activities give this free time an inherent value, even if this value is not nominally recorded.

Yet the act of measuring the rational value of this free time can give that free time a new value. While opportunities will be lost, they will be exchanged for nominal rewards including money and job experience etc. The choice to exchange this free time for nominal rewards like money can be done from a relationship of full and fair agreement, duress or silent consent. Nominal measurement of the value and conditions of this exchange will be determined by the assumptions of the business cycle. Employment standards will determine a minimum wage and relevant unions may determine the going wage rate. Safety standards will determine work practices. Unwritten cultural practices will vaguely determine the social niceties. But the defects of the business cycle will also be a problem. The worker may be asked to work for an economy with spiralling debt issues, with prescribed pension plans that have dubious long term stability. The nominal society he works with may have objectionable moral practices such as onshore or off shore slavery which the worker would rather not participate in. The business cycle may have discriminatory practices or attitudes against his religion, ethnicity, politics or sexuality. He may not like the general culture of the business cycle, feeling that it lessens his personal happiness. He may require debt laden investments such as clothing, certification or transportation to work.

A multitude of issues relates to this simple task of having the value of his free time measured nominally. These will not all be negative. He may also enjoy the camaraderie of working within the culture of the business cycle or feel the joy of self-actualization, the joy of being the best that you can be. Everyone who joins the business cycle does so by choice, whether that choice is of full and fair agreement, duress or silent consent. Full and fair agreement is a consideration of both the parties of all the relevant issues.

In the case of a young adult spending his free time, full and fair consideration is a likely scenario. The worker is young and alert. The free time is discretionary. The employer is likely

Introducing Economic Actualism

hiring non-essential surplus staff so there is no duress on his part.

Yet despite full consideration, surprises can always happen. Economic collapse could erode the value of wages earned or the company pension plan. On the employer's side the employee or a member of his family could have an unknown or undiscovered health condition that could suddenly hinder his work employment. The failure to account for unknown surprises lessens the extent and value of a full and fair agreement, but not the spirit. Assessing such issues through full and fair consideration reduces the uncertainty.

Measuring the rational value of the spare time occurs when nominal rewards are considered. The free time is given a new value by the assumptions of the business cycle including attitudes on ethnicity, politics, religion and sexuality, the value of certification, the value of unskilled labour and assumptions about the long term prospects of the economy as a whole. If the employee finds his time valuation is higher within nominal measurement than without, he will likely chose nominal employment knowing that he may meet surprises. Otherwise, he may maintain his free time outside of nominal measurement.

While the exact percentage is hard to determine, full and fair agreement constitutes what is probably the minority of transactions, especially in a dysfunctional economy. Full and fair consideration is a process that can take leisure time, discretionary income and education. Discretionary income is often a small percentage of total income. The majority of income is often spent on essentials such as housing and transportation and insurance. On these transactions, the buyer may feel that he is under duress, that he has been locked in to his choice by his previous decisions, the decisions of his ancestors or the decisions of his government and his society. For example, the young adult may prefer the idea of driving an electric bike rather than a car, but feels the prevalence of automobiles on the road and the high mortality rate of cyclists when cars and bikes collide, make driving an electric bike impractical. This combined with a perceived inadequacy of public transit, forces him to buy an automobile with a debt he can not afford in a society he believes has too much debt all ready. He thus becomes one more car in a car obsessed culture he despises. He is quite vocal about this. He has thought it through and has told his objection to anyone that will listen. But he has bought an automobile.

© Bobby Deal – Dreamstime.com

Figure 22 Duress can take numerous forms such as rent, food on the table or taxation but it induces irrationality in all. Often, the one who seems to have a gun to our head has a gun to her head and is under duress as well.

More common than duress is the situation of consent through silence. Old habits die hard and when we make one hundred decisions every week, the majority of them are done in silence and without consideration. In 'quiet desperation" we act like cogs in the gears of the social machine paying bills we can not afford and working for wages we can not live with. Knowing that there must be a better way but, in fear that change could also bring about ways that are much worse than the present, we keep the status quo. Sometimes this status quo just seems like a slow death by absurd means, but this seems preferable to a sudden death by violent means.

Free markets require that decisions be made with full and fair consideration. The ability to assess an economic transaction before entering it is a requirement of laissez faire economics. Laissez faire economics, which supposes that economies work best when they are not interfered with, seems increasingly like an unrealistic utopian dream in the modern society. Many social forces restrict consideration. Monopolies, government regulations, anomie, ignorance and social problems can change the economy from one of full and fair consideration to duress and consent by silence. Monopolies force all buyers to purchase from a single source and all suppliers to sell through a single outlet. This bottleneck can restrict feedback forcing decisions to be made by duress and consent by silence. Government regulations can create monopolies also. But they can also restrict feedback.

Anomie is the situation where life is so busy, with so many choices, that you have no leisure time to select a decision properly and life becomes a situation of duress or consent by silence. Ignorance can hinder decision making. Modern society can have so many choices, each of which has so much complexity, that full and fair consideration becomes increasingly rare. Social problems such as substance abuse, discrimination or intolerance can also restrict decision making.

These processes increase the uncertainty of an economy and make the business cycle one of increasing cancerous instability. Decisions made with full and fair consideration are those where the market value of a product is in line with the actual value of that product. People choose to place their good or service within the nominal economy because they have assessed that its value within the nominal economy is more than it is outside of the nominal economy. This is true even in a duress laden society like a dictatorship. In a totalitarian dictatorship they may face the choice of revealing personal information about their friends or colleagues for money, or face punishment or prison. Such a choice may be laden by monopoly, regulation, anomie and social problems, but it is still a choice that is made by weighing the cost of measuring versus not measuring. Outside of nominal measurement, this friendship, the value of a free society and the value of a conscience that gives self-worth all have a value which is weighed against the costs of prison time and the rewards of monetary compensation.

Outside of the nominal measurement, all of these things have value. But once the situation of nominal measurement arises, the rationality all of these items attain different values. A business cycle in which the act of nominal measurement tends to increase the value of life, the summation of goods and services, is one which is stable. A business cycle in which the nominal value is less than the actual value before measurement is unstable.

The process by which decisions move from full and fair consideration towards duress and consent by silence is one which increases uncertainty. One of the problems with consent by silence is that there is little discussion about what is actually going on and so every dictator can claim to have an air of benevolence. While economic uncertainty is not a guarantee of instability, economic certainty in the name of full and fair disclosure can be seen as a guarantee of stability. If people are free to speak their minds and freely chose, they are showing on a daily basis that the nominal economy improves actual living conditions. If they, instead, must rely on monopolies which

Introducing Economic Actualism

suffer social problems to tell them their lives are improving without feedback, the system is prone to cancerous instability.

This instability may not occur immediately. And this can give a false sense of security to the "benevolent dictator" which increases their peril in the long run. As we have seen earlier, while consent is a source of uncertainty, deviations are certain to occur. They are inevitable.

Inversion and ineffectiveness, when they combine in an atmosphere of duress are like fuel, oxygen and a spark: they combine to create fire as illustrated in Figure 23. This economic fire can destroy both the individual life and the society.

SOURCES OF UNCERTAINTY

While fuel, oxygen and a spark are certain to cause a fire, the forces that cause a flock of birds to fluctuate between left and right, or a society to fluctuate between competitive political ideals, are uncertain. Duress acts as a spark to start the economic bubble, yet its silence can make its early stages like a small burning garbage can in the back of an abandoned warehouse. When the fire is noticed, it can be difficult to determine the cause. We must however, isolate and discuss the sources of uncertainty, the social factors that move us from relationships of full and fair consideration towards duress and consent by silence.

A relationship of full and fair consideration is one where both parties feel the value of their rational behaviour is increased by economic participation. Relationships of duress or silent consent are those where one or both parties feel that economic participation decreases the value of their goods or services. Business cycles can start off as full and fair consideration but then increasingly become duress or silent consent as the business cycle progresses. No full and fair consideration is perfect and the forces of ineffectiveness, discussed earlier, will tend to entrap those imperfections so that they can't be corrected until the entire business cycle completes. Yet the bursting of "the bubble" will create a new business cycle which is guided by an altered set of assumptions to facilitate transactions.

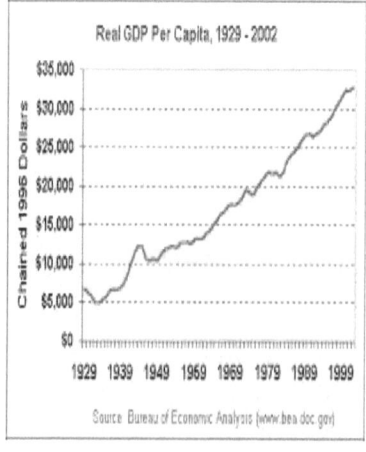

© Maa – Illustrations – Dreamstime.com

Figure 23 Economic deviation can be analogized to the creation of fire.

During this process, the act of economic measurement can measure rational behaviour as being irrational and irrational behaviour as being rational. Duress occurs. And those who are overwhelmed by the complexity or the emotional impact of the business cycle's errors find themselves in situations of quiet desperation. They long desperately for an alternative business cycle, yet lack the words and knowledge to express this longing. A cancerous instability, or bubble, is created which expands until the economy's nominal statistics are so far removed from actuality that the bubble bursts. A new business cycle forms with a new full and fair consideration. However, this transition is usually laden with conflict and often violence. And the damage from the old business cycles, including environmental damage and resentment from conflict, never totally goes away.

The term "quiet desperation" was credited to philosopher Henry David Thoreau. In his book "On Walden Pond", he describes his experiment with living the simple life in rural Massachusetts in the early 1800's. He lived outside of society in a simple shack, growing his own food in a shack. He surmised that a man really needs only four essentials to live a happy life: food and water, shelter, clothing and fuel for cooking and warmth. These are the four needs which man looks to his society for provision. Thoreau carried a shotgun with him on his daily walks, which, though he never used it, felt he should have it in case of need. And of course he read and wrote. These last two items we can consider to be acquired needs, they are needs which we acquire as a result of social interaction which will be discussed later.

But any denial of these four essential items: food and water, shelter, clothing, fuel can cause a situation of duress. We require each of these items on a daily basis for our survival. Thoreau claimed that most of mankind can be said to live in "quiet desperation". The duress is the "desperation" part and the consent by silence is the "quiet" part.

We look to community interaction and economic participation to provide citizens with the essentials of life. Providing these essentials in an economical manner is the economy's primary task. Creating inversions, inefficiencies, idolatries and cancerous instability is not, though many governments seem to confuse such increases of nominal wealth with governance. These deviations are certain to occur. The result of these deviations, where nominal wealth is inverse to actual wealth, is usually econo-addiction: the obsession with promoting economic deviation. This requires economic growth, for relying on a percentage of growing nominal wealth while actual wealth is decreasing can only be maintained by expansion of the business cycle, then flipping a fraction of this nominal expansion into actual rewards for a minority. This requires either geographic, demographic or societal expansion of the economy. Either new lands must be conquered. More people within a society must participate economically or, if the same number participate, they must participate more fully. This process of expansion has limits of course. As a result, nominalist business cycles are inherently unstable and all cancerous instabilities face periods of periodic contraction and adjustment.

While we can be certain economic deviations of the second principle will expand the business cycle in a certain direction, the uncertainty created by the economic measurement of the first principle affects the ability of the business cycle to expand by creating uncertainty and thus, increasing instability. The process of economic measurement reacts with deviations with uncertain results. As duress reduces the rationality of participants, the manner by which the deviations are resolved can be irrational as well.

THE PROCESSES OF DURESS

Economies, especially those with deviations, try to expand. This is often done by means of duress, either accidentally or intentionally. Though this duress is not as certain to occur as deviation is, it is an important source of uncertainty, and thus instability. Four essential needs exist: food including water, clothing, housing and fuel. The provision of any one of these, when they are in critically short supply, entices people to join the economy and promotes economic growth. This is not a secret when it occurs and the people joining the economy can be quite vocal either with approval or disapproval. But it is a source of uncertainty.

When one commodity or service entices people to engage in a vast array of other goods and services, the process of economic measurement can be warped. It is a cliché that the Roman Empire existed in its later days by providing "bread and circuses'". The bread was the provision of basic food. Rome's famous aqueduct system also brought them water. The circus was not a means of duress but a means to provide distraction from critical conversation which created consent by silence through lack of feedback. This cliché is an example of how a society can grow by these two methods. The Irish potato famine in the late 1800's persuaded a large portion of Irish society to come to North America. The availability of farmland was crucial to the settlement of North America. Yet these settlers often had policies of deliberately starving the native populations such as the slaughter of buffalo or John A MacDonald, the first Prime Minister of Canada, trying to reduce native food supplies. These actions were meant to subject natives into the emerging economy. Centralized agriculture is thought to have had a persuasive influence on the expansion of Mayan civilization and also to have played a major role in its collapse which the soils became depleted. Modern Los Angeles, the base of a lot of modern culture, is largely a result of aqueduct systems which bring water to an arid region. People will alter their entire lifestyle, and those of their descendants, if it exchanges them for food when it is scarce.

Yet this can skew the process of economic measurement in uncertain ways. It can allow people to overvalue the other aspects of the society. Yet it can also create resentment and violent undertones.

© Ralf Kraft – Dreamstime.com

Figure 24 In North America during the 1800's, buffalo were hunted so that they went from vast herds across the American prairies to the brink of extinction, which vastly destroyed the food supplies and cultures of many tribes.

The rational acceptance of one critical item such as food can lead to the adoption of many other, less rational items. Fuel is perhaps the most prevalent means of modern duress. Our

Introducing Economic Actualism

modern society consumes vast and exponentially expanding quantities of energy which were once cheap but which are now becoming more expensive. We fight wars over oil. Create communities around pipelines. We make energy into major political issues. Yet these decisions are constant sources of argument. We may want the energy. But many of us resent what it does to our taxation and our quality of life. While these effects are uncertain, they are powerful.

Housing is the cause of many an economic "bubble". People need shelter from the elements and modern housing is a substantial cause of financial obligations. This financial obligation can trap us into lifestyles we resent but can not change. A mortgage can be the modern equivalent of serfdom. Housing also must be serviced by infrastructure supplying other needs such as water and fuel. The acceptance of our housing persuades us to accept a vast array of other lifestyle choices including our community and our source of income.

In modern society, clothing is a key ingredient fuelling the Globalization of the economy. Unlike fuel or housing, clothing is relatively easy to transport and store. The western economies have increasingly looked to less developed countries to supply clothing without the scrutiny of western labour laws. This rationalizes an entire group of arrangements which would otherwise be rejected. The child labour of many of these sweat shops would be condemned if they were localized in more visible locations.

These four items: food including water, housing, fuel and clothing are essential needs that men look to their society to provide. So why should we care? Society provides them under a free market and the price is set by an invisible hand of supply and demand. However, the existence of duress in an economic system can affect the measurement of rational behaviour, not just for the essential item, but for all items in the economy. This is a source of unbiased uncertainty, it can skew measurements but not in a predetermined direction. It can also be a source of instability.

Providing an essential need, which people purchase under a sense of duress, can prevent both positive feelings and resentment. Duress is a situation which leads to irrationality. It is dangerous to save a drowning man, not just because of the water. A drowning man's arms thrash violently and in his panicked state he can view his would be rescuer as a threat. Both men can drown.

© Benoit Daoust – Dreamstime.com

Figure 25 When people are in emergency situations they are less rational and lose objectivity.

While a society in dire need may not be immersed in water, it can be immersed in panic. People who provide disaster relief can be viewed as saviours or as opportunists. So long as no violence occurs, and people are allowed to voice their duress, this panic is an acceptable and important part of business. In non-emergency situations, people may lament the price of housing, the rising price of fuel or food, but if demand is high and supply low, the high price is unavoidable and we can only hope that people will devise ways to lower demand and raise supply.

When an economy supplies one item under duress, it creates uncertainty not only in the consumption of that crucial product, but in the entire economy. The exaggerated gratitude, or resentment, for that needed product effects the valuations of all products in that economy in uncertain ways. We earlier looked at how tulip bulbs became an idol in Holland and how people at the peak of the tulip business cycle would trade a piece of prime real estate for a single tulip bulb. This can be seen as a response to the potato as a commodity that solved the need for northern Europe's need for food. Before Europe's global exploration, northern Europe lacked a crop which could be grown locally that supplied a high yield of calories per acre. The potato, which was introduced to Europe from South America along with the tomato, changed the demographics of northern Europe by allowing high amounts of calories to be produced in colder climates. This created a population explosion. But like a drowning man in a situation of rescue, Europe did not respond rationally to this situation of duress, creating both opportunities and disasters.

This intense need for one item in an economy can increase the participation in an entire economy, increasing the demand for some other products as well, while decreasing the valuation of different goods. When people participate in a business cycle, they tend to consume a complete package of goods, services and assumptions. They may have some differences here and there, buy a little more of this and less of that. They may have some differences of opinion. But even in a free society, they participate in a lifestyle. In dictatorships, the choices are fewer.

David Billings

CREATED DURESS

Yet some economies are obsessed with growth. The economic deviations, which grow nominal wealth while decreasing actual wealth, can only maintain actual wealth for those at the beginning by making the pie bigger, and then taking a smaller slice of this bigger nominal pie. As actual losses from nominalism grow, the economy must expand by taking in larger geographical regions, more people or greater participation from the current people. The surest way to compel more people to participate in an economy, if duress does not presently exist, is to create it.

North American history is perhaps the best case study of this phenomenon, not only because there is so much information available but also because North America, after Columbus, is perhaps the society most plagued by created duress in history. Two factors in North America have combined to compel this creation of duress: a relative lack of actual duress and a culture of "economic growth". Created duress, while not specifically named, has in this society been both an unintentional habit and official policy in North America. An absurd example, largely unintentional, was George W. Bush, who just after the terrorist attacks of 911 when panic threatened to overwhelm America, made a public address that it was America's civic duty to "continue buying". Economic growth, even when it did not meet the subject of current duress, was the panacea that would solve all of our problems. But George W. Bush was not alone in his faith in economic growth. This belief is the cornerstone of modern American society. If there is a politician who challenges the wisdom of nominal economic growth, he receives little support or media coverage. All parties tow the line for "economic growth". Our business leaders, churches and schools follow suit, even in the face of popular resentment. Many recognize that America is on the wrong path, but like a train on a railroad there seems to be no other road to take. Our

Introducing Economic Actualism

ineffectiveness, inversions and idolatries have compelled us to expand, and this requires more participation.

The only way to acquire more participation, if a dire need does not exist, is to create duress. In North America, this creation of duress has generally followed a two pronged approach: to create a need for food and clothing amongst the native population while creating a need for housing amongst the immigrant population. To rob the natives of their food supply, the buffalo were driven to the brink of extinction, natives were driven off of their prime agricultural lands in return for agriculturally poor lands. The native traditional farming practices, which were often mostly beans, corn and squash with supplements

© Kentannenbaum – Dreamstime.com

Figure 26 The terrorist attacks on the World Trade Center in New York City on September 11, 2001 resulted in calls for

consumers to "keep spending" to maintain the economy as a form of war time civic duty.

of game in the winter were devastated and natives forced into a situation of duress of accepting food handouts. Charitable attempts to reduce duress from natives' clothing frequently met with handouts of children's blankets contaminated with smallpox. At the present, clothing is primarily an import, raising dependence. In the modern United States, the use of food stamps is at an all time high, while economical supply of food in the manner of dried foods, which can be very nutritious but which promote self sufficiency, are difficult to purchase.

Meanwhile, housing was also turned into a means of duress for the immigrant population. With the exception of the sod house on the

© Cvandyke & cvandyke – Dreamstime.com

Figure 27 The F.D.R. Memorial in Washington D.C. with statues memorializing the breadlines of the 1930's and the starvation and poverty of an Appalachian couple of that time. The hardships of the 1930's still have a strong effect on American culture but have done little to promote the food security of individuals without government assistance.

Canadian prairie, housing became a source not for living, but for investment. Vast immigrant numbers, plus the wide variety of sources, necessitated enforced building codes. Fear of homelessness in latter years is a source of duress that motivates much economic participation and creates bubbles out of stock markets and housing prices alike.

This combination of food shortages for natives and housing shortages of immigrants has created duress that has propelled participation in the American economy, even though that duress was created or exaggerated. The American economy was constantly shipping food overseas from the table scraps of its fat immigrant citizens while those who had descended

© Steve Lovegrove – Dreamstime.com

Figure 28 Fear of homelessness creates irrational behaviour in our economy.

from the first Thanksgiving starved on barren lands. Meanwhile, city life was a constant struggle to meet the mortgage payment in some prescribed "American Dream".

ACQUIRED DURESS

But perhaps the most pernicious form of created duress in modern societies which have motives high on Maslow's Pyramid has become acquired duress, duress that comes not from innate dire needs but from socially produced or perceived needs. We spoke earlier about the four essential needs that Man looks to his society for: food and water, housing, clothing and fuel. This is the simple life that Thoreau espoused. Everything else may be needed, but is mostly a consequence of society, not a provision by it.

© Kongomonkey – Dreamstime.com

Figure 29 Walden Pond is a small body of water near Concord, Massachusetts where Henry David Thoreau lived in a simple shack eating food which he had mainly grown himself for a year.

While Thoreau was a pioneer in non-violent resistance he carried a shotgun with him on his daily walks around Walden Pond. The need for defence is a source of acquired duress. It is a need created by society, not a solution solved by society. Yet needs due to conflict can be very real and a source of deviation as we saw earlier. Yet as a source of duress, it can also compel participation in the economy. Whether it is the young person, walking down the street, who is drafted in the face or an advancing army or the young street kid who buys a handgun in the threat of another street gang, conflict expands an economy. This expansion is in an instable way, however, and the duress can cause valuations of other products that differ from those not under the duress of conflict. Both the young soldier before a battle and the member of a street gang may be prone to spend more on a bar room experience, and less on gardening supplies, than the average citizen.

Thoreau did not list communication as an essential need, though he read extensively and wrote about his simple life on Walden Pond. Like defence, communication is a need that we acquire from society. To many of us, struggling with resentments, loneliness or anxiety, communication can be a dire need. Modern North America probably spends more on entertainment, education and communication than any other society in history. While these needs are not generally as dire as food, there are starving artists who buck this assertion and find a real passion for self-expression that seems irrational to others and fuels a set of valuations that differ from the norm.

Perhaps the most socially acquired form of duress is that of status. Society persuades people that everything, even the essentials of food, shelter and clothing, are not biological necessities but statements of position or achievement. Just as modern North America seems filled with created duress, we also seem to suffer from status symbols as a form of acquired duress. The advertising and marketing industries are shrewd as to what idolatry of the day is the latest status symbol and how to sell it to an eager public. These forms of duress can be very powerful in the minds of the modern consumer. A home is more than a protection from the elements. It becomes a symbol of wealth and an investment which communicates this achievement to future buyers. Cars are more than transportation. Clothing is more than protection.

Everything we buy today has an aura of status attached to it which is more than imaginary. It is a solution to an acquired social problem: how to communicate our position in society nonverbally without being offensive.

Addictions are another form of socially acquired duress which can overshadow the needs for essentials like food, clothing housing or fuel. It is sad that many of us have "irrationally" exchanged the bare essentials for another fix of some substance society has produced. Whether it is alcohol, cigarettes or some new drug, these are forms of acquired duress. Pornography is another example. And while America may not be the unsurpassed leader in the consumption of theses acquired forms of duress, we certainly are in contention. Substance abuse can compel people to participate in the economy while impairing their ability to contribute legally. Crime is often the result.

Organized religion is a form of socially acquired duress. If we believe that God is everywhere, or as atheists if we believe he is nowhere, life as a hermit on Walden Pond allows us that belief in the sanctity of our own mind. Yet the existence of society, and our participation in it, creates in us a need to socialize religion which to some of us is quite dire. This is not an area where modern North America is presently obsessed, though in the 1800's America had much more religious fervour. If we were more spiritual we might suffer from essential and acquired duress less intensely. But socialized religion brings with it a nominalism of its own. For just as economics has both nominal wealth and actual wealth, so religion has both ritualistic spirituality and inner spirituality. The conflict between these two forms of religion has been intense throughout the ages and across the globe, often surpassing economic and political conflict.

Escapism is the last form of acquired duress we shall consider. In an economy of deviation and created and acquired duress which they can not verbalize, some people just want out. This need to escape can seem irrational at times to others. Much of our culture, which would best be spent on providing and acquiring feedback, is instead a form of escapism. Horror films, sci-fi, rock or country music and much of popular culture, can be seen as escapist, or nihilistic. Any cultural escapism can be seen as part feedback, but when it is nihilistic its message can be harder to decipher and less practical than when it deals with issues in a straight forward way.

The vacation industry is largely escapist. Many of us struggle with our jobs, our mortgage and our community all year just for a couple of weeks where we drive our status laden automobiles to the wilderness so we can camp and expose our children to the finer aspects of life. Long weekends are our chance to cook on the grill and have a couple of beers. Or we airplane to a far off island and mingle with the inhabitants of a society which seems more rational to us. Escapism is really a symptom of our inability to deal with the society we live in however. When we suffer consent by silence, escapism is practiced.

THE PROCESSES OF CONSENT BY SILENCE

An economy whose deviations motivate growth can resemble what is commonly called a pyramid structure of marketing. An elite at the beginning are in a constant need of creating subordinates who in turn need subordinates under them and so on. Until, eventually, the market for the proposed good evaporates and those at the bottom of the pyramid, the current crop of new recruits, loses everything while those elites who already climbed to the top walk away. While the previous discussion of duress may lead us to assume that duress applies only to those at the lower levels, those from the beginning stages of the pyramid may actually have the most commitment, and hence the most duress, of anyone in the pyramid. This is important to consider when one looks at consent by silence. It is not only the underlings who are rendered speechless.

When we participate in a business cycle we a buying a complete set of goods, products and assumptions, even if this participation is motivated by only one item under duress. Just as birds in a flock can pulse from side to side in a symmetric unison, so people can pulse from political left to right in an ideological symmetrical unison. But instead of physical position and direction of flight, with people the elements of herding are things like: wages, executive salaries, stock evaluations, real estate prices, fashion trends, media coverage and

© Martin Valigursky – Dreamstime.com

Figure 30 Many of us can not participate in the economy without the occasion escape whether it be a vacation, a second home, the occasional movie, a casino or even a good book.

Introducing Economic Actualism

social etiquette. The list is endless. How birds achieve this symmetry is a mystery. How men achieve this symmetry is not well understood either. But it relies upon selective silence.

There are seven billion people on Earth and something like 35 billion have lived throughout history. Each of us has at least a dozen issues on any given day. The average human mind can only accommodate a couple hundred relationships at any given time, even if we are healthy. Many people can maintain less. And most of us are lucky if we can form an intimate relationship with even one person. Yet we exist within economies of hundreds of millions of people and an emerging global economy which includes all seven billion of us. We may be desperately concerned with our toothache today but the worker in Bangladesh could not care less as he may be concerned with a flood of which we are in turn, unaware and unconcerned. Yet as economies expand, the tooth ached American and flood weary Asian become linked as the Asian makes our shirts.

Just as the flock of birds pulse in unison, the economy we participate in pulses with its topic of discussion. This chosen topic will help determine the social direction. But stronger than the force of deciding what to talk about are the forces that keep men silent. This silence is necessary on a planet crowded with babbling voices. But the stronger this necessity, the more uncertain economic measurement becomes.

Credibility is the source that allows us to speak. Whether it be religious, scientific, moral, legal, conventional, personal or professional, society imbues some of us authority to speak on some topics while asks others to adopt more of a listening role on these specific topics. In a complex society, many subjects require specialization. The religious need to be divine. The scientific need to be knowledgeable and reasoned. Ethical subjects and positions of trust require moral standing. Legal opinions are based on precedent. Old habits die hard. And professional behaviours must meet standards. People who meet these qualifications are often called "authorities" and are given the microphone.

These authorities are one of the idols of modern society. We bow to their talents and experience. We trust them with our lives. We trust them with our children. We let them build our civilization. We pay them, sometimes through taxes. Even in an information age when their degrees are outdated within a couple of years of graduation and when the governments and corporations that support them are constantly in need of assistance, we give special heed to their voice.

Yet the most essential measure of an authority is often the ability to maintain silence. The measure of a modern authority relies not just on his ability to speak regarding his area of specialization. Nominally, an authority is often justified by his ability to avoid certain areas of discussion. We recognize this in politicians constantly. They speak of job creation and wage hikes with one crowd, free commerce with the next crowd. Some will avoid the topic of government debt altogether, though none of them seems to have a solution to it. Before the internet age it was far easier for politicians to practice what Orwell called "double speak".

Two sources of authority exist, actualist and nominalist. Actualist authority comes from a reputation for skill of increasing actual wealth and well-being. This is the form of authority most people recognize and respect. It is a medical doctor's ability to heal. Or it is a clergyman's knowledge of scripture. Perhaps it is a tradesman's ability to build a house properly and on time within budget. Like nominalist authority, actualist authority is a skill that not all have. Though unlike nominalist authority, everyone consciously recognizes actualist authority.

Nominalist authority is the ability to maintain nominal wealth, either of the entire society or of a specific interest group, despite the actual situation. A distinction needs to be made between nominalist authority and criminal negligence.

Criminal negligence is when a doctor knowingly fails to tell a patient he has curable cancer. An example of nominal authority is when a doctor tells the public cancer is best cured by the techniques and pills his trade union is selling rather than prevention or natural cures. Criminal negligence is when a home builder builds on a faulty foundation so that the home collapses five years after purchase. Nominal authority is when the building association uses the fear of faulty foundations to raise union rates and home prices unnaturally. Criminal negligence is enabling a paedophilic clergyman. Nominal authority is searching the scriptures for popular theological distracting sermons. Criminal negligence is embezzling government funds. Nominalist authority tells the public that the economy will grow indefinitely without error regardless of public debt because everyone says that.

The difference between criminal negligence and nominalist authority is crucial, particularly since nominalist authority, while incredibly damaging, is not likely to be illegal. If nominalist authority were illegal, we would all be in jail. Nominalist authority is, in essence, a sort of silence which afflicts both the "respected authority" and the "common novice". While people may look to authorities for guidance against nominalism, this would be a mistake. The authorities in their respected fields are usually under more duress regarding the defects of their specialization than anyone else. The medical profession for instance, is not perfect. Hundreds of thousands of people in the Unites States die every year from medical mistakes. Prescribed pharmaceuticals have side effects. Some, like Thoreau, feel that food and natural living will prevent most diseases which the medical profession has turned into an industry that is consuming the economy. But like most of us, doctors do not talk about this much. And actually, considering that they talk about medicine all day

David Billings

Figure 31 Legally, the difference between criminal negligence and acceptable mistake is of adherence to "common standards of practice". If everyone else is doing the same mistake, it is excused. Yet when an actual disaster does occur, such as this bridge failure, it will be a cause of nominal economic growth.

long, they probably talk less about disease prevention than the common man if a percentage of time regarding talk of medicine is considered.

Yet unlike the common novice, the medical professional is under a great deal of duress about the nominal abilities of his profession. A certified doctor had to earn top marks, spend top dollars and spend years in advanced education including a year of deprived sleep in residency. His professional association, which is really just a union, is made up of people with similar histories dealing with complex topics. His high pay is necessary to offset his costs, but when he chose medicine as a career, he chose a complete set of variables. Some aspects of his profession he approved of. Some he did not. But he bought all of them. And after years of debt and studying nothing else, he has a vested interest in the profession's assumptions. He also has a specialization in them to the neglect of other fields.

Thoreau and Plato may have had a point about the virtues of natural medicine but if you are having extreme pain in your chest, or some other emergency, you are better off at the hospital rather than talking to a philosophy graduate. As a novice you have doubts about the medical profession, but you are in an emergency, a situation of duress. You submit yourself to the emergency ward. You are purchasing the entire medical system: a labyrinth of procedures, tests and pills you know nothing about. You may be abnormally grateful. You may be resentful. But you practice consent by silence, as do the nurses and doctors.

Other professions face similar challenges of nominalism. If your toilet backs up you call a plumber. But he is unlikely to mount a political campaign to separate the storm and sanitary sewer systems. You go to church on Christmas day but keep your reservations about some controversial topic to yourself. You talk to your local politician about one matter that concerns you but do not mention an array of other topics. Such actions are part of the political process and are a form of consent by silence. You can only talk about one issue at a time.

When one item entices you to participate in an economy under a situation of duress, you give consent to a wide variety of other goods and services through your silence. You fall in love. You get married and get a mortgage. The mortgage requires both of you to get jobs. The stress causes both of you to gain weight. Your kids go to school. Thanks to the enormity of your mortgage payments you tend to view other costs as being insignificant and spend more than you otherwise would. You remain constantly in debt. Your health suffers. You hardly find time for your spouse anymore and your marriage, your motivation for the whole lifestyle in the first place, fails. It is a common example of consent by silence in our modern society. One item in duress leads to consent to many other items.

This process of consent by silence effects everyone, from the common novice to the respected expert. Though people tend to listen to him more, the respected expert may be under more duress and suffer consent by silence more than the rest of us. But other factors other than duress affect this consent through silence.

Being part of the division of labour is a big factor, though this is also a form of duress. Having an intense specialization can give you a lack of knowledge of other truth and other lifestyles. Dedication to a cause is not only a source of duress. It is also a source of inability to speak on alternative philosophy.

An inability to communicate is a major source of consent by silence. This is not only a matter of literacy, but in a modern society, it is also a matter of having access to the instruments of communication. This is one area where respected authorities have an advantage in that their position tends to give them more access. But this tendency is less than you might expect. Modern society often gives more access to the media for the bimbo with plastic surgery that the gawky, senior professional with a startling revelation.

Complexity and anomie, the situation of having too many choices, increase the demands on our communication and learning abilities. We inevitably are silent on more topics, though we devote the same amount of time and effort to our speech.

Chapter Four

Social Confusion

We live in an age of exploding information. We are awash with new data. Our schooling is obsolete within years of graduation. Encyclopaedias are instantly out of date. We get news from all over the world. Data exists on everyone, everywhere all the time. We spend increasing amounts of our lives in school.

© Iqoncept- Dreamstime.com

Figure 32 Despite the vast amounts of information available, many of us are more confused than ever.

Yet we are confused. Our politicians tell us our economy is growing. Our advertisements tell us we are better serviced than anyone in history. Our medical profession tell us we are living longer. Yet to many, our lives are not so wise, but hectic. Not learned but studying or practicing. Not rich, but indebted. Not free, but committed. Not at peace, but at war with weapons too terrible to use. We have confused actual with nominal wealth, and we have done so flamboyantly, with bravado, and on a grand scale. It paid well, or so we thought.

We seek actual wealth. Nominal wealth is just a necessary tool we use to create actual wealth. We create nominal wealth, then "flip it" to obtain actual wealth. But nominal wealth is a form of lie, a very powerful one. After the journey which starts by a situation of actual duress and which proceeds through created duress, acquired duress and deviation, many of us have forgotten what actual wealth is. Just as people must use power saws carefully to avoid being injured, so we must use nominalism carefully, minimizing it as best as we can. While power saws are approached with caution, economic nominalism is often used with complete abandon of reserve. For the "love of money is the root of all evil" for which purpose men will" subject themselves to numerous afflictions".

Rather than creating nominal wealth and then using that nominal wealth to obtain actual wealth, the actualist objective is to create actual wealth in the first place. Economic actualism tries to eliminate the nominal stepping stone. This sounds easier than it is. Inversion, ineffectiveness, idolatry and duress make it difficult and the human dependence upon society for essentials make this a permanent problem. Just as we all have sinned, so too, we all have created worthless nominal wealth with the unstated goal of flipping it for actual benefit. The actualist is lucky if he only manages to reduce his nominalist tendencies.

Much of our social discourse, from our political discussion to our study of history to our social commentary, to our popular media to our clinical psychology to our economic theory is fixated on this juxtaposition of the nominal mask which we place over the actual truth. The fixation is stronger for the fact that the concept is undefined. It is the needs we can not verbalize which gnaw at our subconscious. Much like sublimated sexual desires, our needs for actual wealth and our need to abandon nominalism can control our thoughts and behaviours more than we realize.

This lack of realization, when placed within the confines of a herd mentality, makes us extremely vulnerable to nominalism. But we don't realize it. These effects of nominalism can reach our very core. While many economic decisions, such as newlyweds in search of a home, can be seen as sexually motivated, many sexual desires and dysfunctions may be caused by nominalism. The unspoken frustrations and manic episodes caused by nominalism are not verbalized by us. Nominalism may prolong periods of duress giving us free floating anxieties we can not diagnose or treat. Nominalism may also give us feelings of success we secretly feel we do not deserve but can not express: a recipe for depression. Nominalism may fill actualists in us with uncontrolled rage or give us obsessions. While economics is in itself a dreary subject, its outcomes effect lives and can have emotional impacts, especially when nominalism can persuade us to waste large portions of our life.

LEFT RIGHT CONFUSION

While we don't see it, much of our political debate is steeped with the problems of nominalism. The political paradigm of "left versus right" which has dominated western democracy is a situation where both sides carry out a nominal agenda they can not verbalize. Advancing nominal wealth is an uncontested objective for both sides. Meanwhile both sides criticize the failures of the other to achieve actualist objectives. This criticism seems to be spurred on by each opposing side's failure to recognize the dedication and hardship which nominalism requires of the other. It is a cycle whose viciousness is unchecked because of its unrecognized cognitive dissonance as will be described in "The Politics of Economic Actualism".

The left versus right debate is in many ways a parallel of the cold war. The political left tends to favour big government and wealth redistribution. The political right tends to support smaller government, less taxation and free enterprise supported by populist habit and culture.

In the cold war, the Soviet Union and their allies followed Marx who wrote critically of the "robber barons". The robber barons could best be summarized as people who used the need for individuality of the free enterprise to exploit workers. On the other side of the cold war was the United States and their allies who followed free market economists. These free market economists criticize followers of Marx as "communists", people who used government and the need for communal life to exploit and rob the electorate.

I have never personally met any one who called themselves a "robber baron" or a "Communist". While Marx himself used the word communist in his title "The Communist Manifesto", it is a term that has largely gone into obscurity since the Soviet Union went bankrupt. However, these two groups were bitterly divided and could not speak to each other. Their division was basically on how to divide the spoils of nominal economic wealth. Both, seeing the frustration and desperation of their own camps in terms of actual wealth, saw the errors of nominalism in the other and were critical.

While many of us would argue that communism has become an irrelevant theory, its recent shadow of governing one third of the global population in the 1980's and its long standing influence in the technological age still affects our culture. Much of the left-right paradigm in western politics still has roots in this conflict.

This controversy continues to a lesser degree in the left – right paradigm of western politics. Both political ideals are united in their belief in the nominalist goal, such as expanding the economy, they just disagree violently about how to create

Introducing Economic Actualism

this expansion and also how to divide the spoils. But there is little critical analysis of what this expansion is made of or what motivates it. The need for this expansion seems to be an idol so central to society that it can not be questioned.

This inability to see a problem is a red flag symptom in addictions such as drug addiction or alcoholism. It is a red flag symptom that an addictive relationship may have formed. In the case of the left – right paradigm, both parties deny that they are suffering an addiction, to nominal economic growth, but instead blame their misfortune on their social partner. Like an alcoholic married couple who constantly bicker over the other's minor infractions, they fail to question the value of their alcohol. The alcohol was how they dated. It was how they married and honeymooned. Without the alcohol, nothing much holds their marriage together. So both spouses irrationally blame the other for their misery.

The modern right left paradigm is analogous to this contentiously drunken married couple. If the left represents big government and trade organizations and the right represents free business, then these two are inextricably linked, or married, in a modern economy. Business needs government to provide services. Since people don't conform perfectly they need schools and roads, etc. And government needs independent production. Attempts by business to totally eradicate government and its services to support the estranged simply replace the current government with a substitute government. In a short time it will closely resemble the old government. And any government effort to nationalize everything, or use government resources to change actual behaviour from above will, in time, needs to allow independent actions to meet new demands under customs of their own choice. A business cycle needs both team play based upon common nonverbal agreement and individuality based upon expression.

The government is best thought of as collection of resources while free enterprise enables us to produce through collective habit. The relationship between the individual and the collective is in all human activity. Its paradigm comes from man's dependence on centralization. Yet it also comes from centralization's inverting effects. Though the name "Collectivist-Individualistic Paradigm" is not used, it is closely related to the right left paradigm.

Dependence on centralization is the one source of deviation without an absolutely desirable direction. People do not need no centralization. They do not need complete centralization. They need the amount that is just right, even though dependence on centralization is a source of deviation. A children's soccer team has both individual and team efforts. Likewise a steel mill has both individual effort in optimizing labour and it has collective work; management to assign tasks and organize the individual efforts of salespeople. A government office has both individual efforts to adapt their service to unique cases and a changing society, and a collective effort to control the disbursement of funds.

One of the most damaging confusions of this right left paradigm is the belief that if you are a leftist, accused of being a communist, that you can not be accused of being a robber baron. And if

© Apartura – Dreamstime.com

Figure 33 A children's soccer team has both team and individual efforts just as adult societies inescapably have both accomplishments from team work and from individual initiative.

you are a rightist, who is being accused of being a robber baron, then you can not be accused of being a communist. This situation seems a symptom of the latter days of econo-addiction, when all of us struggle with the multiple and often contradictory mental processes we are required to use when we live in both the actual and nominal world. It is really a form of anarchism, giving left wingers the freedom to indulge in being robber barons and right wingers the freedom to be communists without criticism. Yet human existence fates "the right" to serve a collective in the name of collectivism and "the left" to serve individuals in the name of individualism as described in "The Politics of Economic Actualism".

Government workers can intrapreneur, run their section of the government like a private kingdom, yet remain free from criticism. From the insecure high school teacher who peeves students yet is free from criticism as long as he sticks to government curriculum to the bureaucrat that works bankers' hours and has lavish expense accounts, leftists can adopt an anarchistic immunity to criticism for nominalized individual effort in their stated quest for individualism to actualists.

Likewise, a collective of right wingers can exploit the public need for community without criticism. In the name of national defence, the military industrial complex can sell $50 dollar toilet seats and billion dollar aircraft in the name of the common good, all without fear of being engaged in collective "or Communist" behaviour which exploits workers in the cause of nominalist growth. In both these situations, the set of ethics by which the party sells itself to actualists is trampled. But the damage is excused, so long as it advances the nominalist cause. Our existence is like this.

The left-right paradigm of belief is best explained as a collectivist-individualist paradigm, where the left expresses the individualistic mentality with its tolerance and redistribution and the right expresses the commoditizing needs of society that rely on conformity. It can also be described, as it is in "The Psychology of Economic Actualism" as a tradesman-artist paradigm where the right commoditizes production to enable individuals while the left allows individuals to express their individuality. These two distinct mentalities are interdependent but contradictory.

Society needs both collectivism and individualism. This situation results because we need centralization, yet it is a form of inversion. Relationships of collectivism join us into teams and communities. Collectivism, as naïve actualism, creates data under rules. These rules create a common habit. They provide laws and customs. They create moral obligations to take care of the weaker members of the collective. In collectivism, all people in a society contribute in some way to the common good. The wealthy would not be wealthy without a class of less wealthy who support them. Wealth is made within a business cycle of habits. And since all contribute in a collective society, all deserve to have a share in the wealth generated by that society as long as they conform. Yet bad experiences persuade us in time away from collectivism towards the nominal rewards of a collective.

The left tends to break from the conformity of the business cycle and tends to see redistribution as a remedy to the collective's misdeeds. They sell this to actualists by pitching individualism, but over time, bad experiences force them to sell the nominal rewards of specific individuals. But the collectivist often resents the wealth of the rich individualist, even if it was gained by solving crises of genuine duress. The individual can break the unwritten code the collectivist lives by.

People of the left can view this individualism with an almost religious fervour. The passion can exceed that of their religious faith as to them, the collectivist ideologies such as communism and most religions are just lies to control poor people by giving them false dreams. To the leftist, individual creativity is the saviour of the poor and the only defence against conformity seeking rightists. This makes accusations of the left acting like the robber barons a heinous taboo, even though their inability to commoditize themselves often requires assistance from others such as socialism. But they can not seem to conceptualize taxation, any taxation, as being a form of robbery. When rightists insist that the individual who conforms to quality standards can spend money more efficiently on the poor's behalf than the government slush fund which supports the eccentric, the idea is dismissed without consideration.

The right is collectivistic or team oriented and thus gains freedom from minor conformities. A society which tries to control everything into conformity is oppressive, stagnant and creates a lifestyle which is not worth living. Collectivism gives us productivity, though it may be within a set of a business cycle's assumptions which they would rather the individualists not challenge. Individualism allows society to adapt. New companies may in the end, be gobbled up by corporate conglomerates, but they often start off in garages as a simple idea from an eccentric. In the eyes of individualism, wealth is created, not by a collective, but by individuals who are not constrained by habits and centralized institutions.

The team players usually rely heavily on a set of assumptions which is unexpressed however. The nuisance of expression and verbalization of concepts is often left to the leftists. The team players or individualists have a business cycle in their minds eye which, through its conservatism, receives widespread and silent consent. If everyone just consented to this unwritten code, government regulation and long winded rhetoric would be largely unneeded.

Taxation in this view is a form of crime, which rewards the unproductive and penalizes the productive. But these labels of "productive" and "unproductive" are seen through the unquestioned lens of the business cycle, a self imposed form of blindness. To socialists, the business cycle can purposely blind itself to the damages it causes and needs taxation, education and redistribution just as the blind need glasses and a white cane. Philosophies of individualism create needs for collectivism while collectivist philosophies give rise to the need for individuals. Marx himself, was an individual bucking the establishment of his time who believed that, in an eventual recession, unemployed workers would just refuse to leave the factory because they had no where else to go.

The military industrial complex constantly invents new weapons upon the inspiration of individuals, but does so with collectivist goals of preservation and expansion of the state. Yet just as the left can not consider their actions to be those of robber barons, so the right can not consider that their actions are at times communistic. But the stock market is a collectivist centralization of power which, through its often monopolistic power, prevents many citizens from fully exerting their individualism.

Ironically, many rightists seem to like to see themselves as "robber barons" because they see their success as unquestionable signs of their individuality, when their success is essentially that of going farther in the business cycle than anybody else. Many leftists like to see themselves as collectivists, even communists, as unquestionable recognition that their struggles to exert their individuality were for the common good, rather than an obsessive avoidance of commoditizing themselves. Each mentality uses different classes of symbols yet a specious pride in social involvement can permeate all mental processes originating from their zealotry. Human existence is a constant struggle against confusion between different mindsets.

The people on the right are offended by "communists", those who exploit society's need to live as a collective for their own personal needs, perhaps because they feel themselves fighting similar temptations. People on the left are offended by "robber barons" because they fight such temptations on a daily basis. However, these two tendencies are the modes by which these two philosophies tend to fail as a result of their existence. So they feel a bit of pride if the opposite failure is labelled upon them, especially as the label is often erroneous.

This constant argument between collectivism and individualism is inescapable. Centralization of power is a form of economic deviation. Activities can be carried out by individuals that, outside of the central economy, generate actual wealth but not nominal wealth. Likewise, activities of the central government such as digging holes and then refilling them can generate nominal but not actual wealth. But unlike other inversions, we need some centralization.

The discourse is clouded as both rightists and leftists deny the nominalism in themselves at some times and deny their actualism at other times. They see actualism as vestiges of their own childhood, nominalism as symptoms of decay. They deny both. Leftists who refuse to see the possibilities of themselves as robber barons and rightists who refuse to see communism in themselves are both the result of Marx's central thesis, that human history is a story of "class conflict". The classes use different mentalities that need each other in a love-hate relationship.

Just as capitalism arose out of Man's need to "dominate nature" and actualism is arising due to the "confusion of actual and nominal wealth", communism arose from perceived "class conflict". The robber barons were, for their own individual benefit, exploiting the collective efforts of the workers. This situation results from the cognitive dissonance between six contradictory mental processes we all need as described in the upcoming "The Politics of Economic Actualism".

This concept of "class conflict" has poisoned the public discourse. As we discussed earlier, conflict is inevitable. Everyone, all the time, conflicts with each other in one form or another. Siblings fight. Spouses fight. Parents and children fight. Nations fight. Childhood soccer teams fight. And yes, business leaders and labourers fight. Marx held that this fight between owners and labourers was central to history and that eventually, the interests of the collective would prevail over the owners to create a "socialist republic" like the Soviet Union or a "People's Liberation Army" in China.

But Marx's obsession with "class conflict" offered no means other than armed struggle to resolve or mitigate the conflict. Other areas of the world invented trade unions to speak for workers and legislation such as minimum wages to mitigate the problem. But the stubborn insistence on conflict trashes the discussion for any discourse. Many communists don't debate well.

While Marxism describes many truths, even today, the obsession with conflict limits the effectiveness of all concerned. When life becomes an all embracing obsession to conquer the robber barons, the individual style players on a soccer team, you can not bear to see a robber baron in yourself or your accomplices. Yet as communist theory rushed headlong to promote collectivism, its needs for individualism increased.

Wearing a collectivist mask all day long, the face behind the mask becomes increasingly individualistic, yet it is a face he can not bear to see. The obsession of the "Communist Manifesto" of bringing communism to the entire globe creates a similar problem for the rightist. The rightist may not use the phrase "economic inversion from centralization of power" to describe communism but he knows that he doesn't like it very much. He may not use the word "collectivism" but he can see tyrants oppressing the population which they swore to liberate, especially when it's a different collective. But when someone is practicing conflict against you and producing weapons you have to take it seriously.

Yet, as the communists are proud to point out, all of us have an innate need to contribute in a social, collectivist manner which can find expression in many forms of communal activity such as cultural or sporting events or something more serious such as political or social rallies.

The "Communist Manifesto", and related doctrines, forces us to repress individualistic expression. But this repression of the individual is futile. By denying our need exists, it goes uncontrolled. The rightist will deny or feel shame from the collectivism within themselves as they have repressed it from their youth. Adult people do not live and fight for "collectivism", they live and fight for a "collective" which often conflicts with other collectives. As nominalists, leftists do not live and fight for individualistic expression, they live and fight for the expression of an individual. This is described in "The Psychology of Economic Actualism" and the upcoming "The Politics of Economic Actualism" as people become nominalists and shun actualism as they "mature".

This reaction can be sublimated into idolatry. The only way to express this violent need in a way accepted by the society is by surrendering to a higher power. Excessive surrender to a central power is not only a form of economic inversion, it is also motivates idolatry and econo-addiction.

Alcoholics Anonymous has a twelve step program to deal with addiction. The first step is to admit your addiction. The second step is to surrender to a higher power. Under the current right left paradigm, with its declaration of irreversible conflict, both left and right struggle with nominalism as it pulls the right from collectivism towards the interest of a collective and it pulls the left from individualistic expression towards that of individuals' expression.

David Billings

© Embe2006 – Dreamstime.com

Figure 34 Stock markets indexes such as the Dow Jones Industrial Average nominalize the collective efforts of individuals as the well being of dictators nominalizes the individualistic efforts of a collective.

If economics is the study of rational behaviour as an ideal then politics is the study of community irrationality, specifically the resolution of cognitive dissonance amongst populations. Dissonance is a feeling of disharmony like a musical chord that sounds off. Cognitive dissonance is the disharmony between separate and distinct mental processes.

As described in "The Psychology of Economic Actualism" our existence as members of Mankind is a struggle between six mental processes, which we desperately need in order to provide the essentials of our lives. But these mental processes contradict each other, do not understand each other and as a result, they do not like each other. They oppose each other, repel each other and yet are dependent upon each other both within the same polis and within the same mind. The left right paradigm is perhaps the most prominent form of cognitive dissonance, particularly as portrayed in modern media, though it is not the only form.

Briefly, each mental process has both contradictory methods and contradictory objectives. But what really confuses us is that each mental process produces a different and essentially exclusive class of symbols. The tradesman commoditizes himself and produces data. The policeman commoditizes others and produces labels. The artist individualizes and produces opinions. The socializer facilitates listening and produces ideals. The loner produces an unreserved "no" without rationale. The zealot produces an unreserved "yes" without rationale. The gulf between these mental processes and their factions is far greater than that between foreign languages. Yet each class of symbols: data, ideals, money and others all form standards or "currencies".

Different languages share a common objective and similar rules of syntax. All languages seek to provide a standard of communication that will allow individual opinion to be socialized into a common culture. They all have similar syntax of concepts like nouns verbs, possession, past tense, adjectives, adverbs and pronouns. All languages have a common goal with similar methods. But they tend to work in different communities, so they are also independent. Different languages arose because their respective communities developed without dependence upon each other.

While we struggle with foreign languages, they do not create cognitive dissonance in the same manner that different mental processes do. The different mental processes are extremely interdependent just as the lungs, the heart and the kidney relate on a constant and intimate basis. But their objectives and methods are contradictory, mysterious and unknown to each other.

The right is largely "ethical" and the left is largely "aesthetic", to use the terms of Kierkegaard. This is a simplification. But different factions tend to prefer different mental skills. Politics is the practice of reducing the cognitive dissonance between these different mental process and their factions as described in "The Politics of Economic Actualism".

CONFUSION FROM CURRENCY ACCEPTANCE

The confusion over left versus right, which is compounded by communist theory, is an example of how the nominalism can create idolatries that are not only above the law but above criticism when guilty of betraying their own stated beliefs, so long as the unspoken idols of nominalism are not endangered. You can break the law and betray your own party's ideal, even traverse social morals and endanger thermonuclear war but as long as you maintain economic growth, all is forgiven.

The essential aspect of nominal economic growth is acceptance of the money supply. Currency acceptance is a central feature of the centralization of power. Fiat currency, like paper money, is a form of communication that gives value to a worthless object. Both selfish and selfless motives exist among authorities for promotion of a currency's use. From a selfish perspective they gain the ability to create seemingly unlimited amounts of wealth out of a worthless product. People will trade their very lives for a currency they accept in the belief that others will accept it as well.

Currency usage can be a form of economic deviation since it can raise nominal wealth while decreasing actual wealth. It increases nominal wealth as currency is the current instrument of economic measurement. Without acceptance of the currency, no nominal records exist at all. When actual wealth decreases from acceptance of a currency, the concurrent nominal increase creates an inversion which is supported by selfish motives of currency creators.

Yet there are selfless motivations as well. For while currency acceptance can be a form of deviation, particularly when motivated by duress and consent by silence which it usually is, centralization of power is the one form of deviation that has benefits. Without currency of some kind, even if it was feathers or smooth pebbles or even kind words, we would be animals. We rely on society to provide the essentials of food, shelter, clothing and fuel and without currency, no society to provide these essentials would exist. Provision of a currency entails great efforts and expenses, the justification for taxation.

The acceptance of a currency is a cause for confusion however. The hallmark of acceptance is that no one questions it. When we buy a hamburger at a fast food restaurant, we don't expect the cashier to haggle with us over whether the currency is valid. Two possible reasons to question a currency's validity exist. It could be counterfeit, not issued by the authorities. Or the authorities themselves may seem invalid. Maybe the country is about to lose militarily. Maybe its justice system is corrupt and people want to limit their exposure to it. Maybe the economy does not sell much that anyone, or at least not much that the person making the evaluation, wants to buy. Or maybe the finances supporting the currency are unstable. If we were to discuss the validity of a currency for every minor transaction, questioning its acceptance, it would be unusable. Currency acceptance requires a lot of consent by silence.

Supposedly, people with authority, maintain the validity of the currency so we can use it without apprehension or quarrel. Yet authority has two sources, actual and nominal. Nominal authority will always be slanted towards currency acceptance. It is an example of society's trend towards speciousness, unwarranted moral authority.

Promoting acceptance of the currency is a major source of consent by silence. A major source of confusion is that an item only has value when it is measured by the currency. It would seem obvious that goods, time and services have an intrinsic value, even if they are not measured by the prevalent currency. But the sheer weight of silence on this fact in a society buzzing with noise to the contrary gives an Orwellian power to the idea that nothing has value until money touches it. This confusion has had a subtle yet powerful influence on society through history.

OTHER PARADIGMS

The current obsession with "diversity" is a similar manifestation of economic growth. Despite the proliferation of the media, modern North America is in many ways intellectually stagnant. Yet there are active campaigns to listen to people of different clothing styles, skin colors, places of origin, religions and sexual orientations. But the interest in these minorities does not seem to be in their intellectuality. This might be generally interesting, particularly from an actualist perspective. Ideas of how people from Africa support and entertain themselves under conditions of poverty might be really useful right now. Or how homosexuals support themselves in their old age without children.

But instead, our current obsession with diversity is how these "different" groups find ways to join the nominalist cause and support the economic growth of the current business cycle, creating another notch in the belt of the current business cycle. Our obsession with diversity is really just an obsession with expanding the current business cycle to new markets with little genuine interest in how that diversity can reform our economy. Like a used car salesman with a desperate mortgage situation who has to sell a lemon, a nominalist at the end of a failing business cycle will say anything and do anything to anyone to extend the nominalist cause. And we are all nominalists.

Every business cycle has a multitude of assumptions that are required to ensure speedy acceptance of the currency and to minimalize or avoid conflict. Yet as the business cycle progresses these assumptions become farther away from actuality, creating confusion. While the effects of the prominent religion on the business cycle are also often avoided, they can be substantial. A Muslim economy that forbids high interest rates and punishes theft severely can differ from a protestant economy that has different attitudes. This is an entirely different topic beyond the scope of this book, but it must be mentioned. Like the left-right paradigm in politics, there is also a ritualistic to spiritualist paradigm to religion, even within worship of the same god or theology.

Religion has often played a role in justifying colonialism, where one country comes to dominate another economically with minimal military force. This is a central paradigm in North American history, as other nations, primarily from Europe, dominated North American culture and economics after Columbus. In many ways, this can be analyzed as the nominalization of North America. It is dangerous to generalize about early North American history. It was host to a multitude of nations with distinct cultures and languages most of which are poorly preserved and some probably have vanished with hardly a trace. The US Navy was founded by pirates, those who sailed an ocean vessel in defiance of European monarchy. The Vikings had settlements before Columbus and though they are reported to have been vacated, no one really knows. The Book of Mormon claims that some of the Israelites emigrated to North America before the captivity in Babylon. Remnants of advanced societies which have been lost can be found all over North and South America, as there are in most areas of the world.

However, history has tended to view the culture of native American as if it was homogenous in what is a classic example of nominal authority. Before Columbus, the Americas had probably hundreds of different cultures and languages which were replaced with primarily four languages from Europe: English, Spanish, French and Portuguese. In European eyes, the various cultures of North America were barbarous and a nuisance. For convenience, the Europeans tended to lump them into one common society. To further avoid discussion, and perhaps to enshrine their appearance of aloofness and stupidity, they labelled the native Americans as "Indians" after a country thousands of miles away and with really no cultural relevance to the situation except that it immortalized Columbus' errors.

However, it would be fair to generalize that for some reason, North America was a much more actualistic group of societies than Europe in 1492. The people of Europe were largely ruled by monarchies which idolized themselves within idolatrous castles. Like most nominalists, Europe had problems living with the confines of their own error and thus found themselves forced to constantly expand. Native America instead had a culture of long range planning incorporating respect for the environment. Both native Americans and Europeans worked with metals but the Europeans had technological superiorities in breastplates and firearms which came from European conflicts creating economic inversions.

The process of economic colonization can be seen as an expanse of nominalism. The combination of created duress and financial obligation expand one country's business cycle to another without martial law being imposed. North America seems to have always felt a moral obligation to accept refugees from nominalist lands. The Statue of Liberty, an iconic symbol of historical sentiment, has an inscription on its base welcoming the "poor and huddled masses, yearning to breathe free". In many instances, such as the first Thanksgiving dinners or when natives taught early settlers to live on bark in the winter, natives were quite supportive of immigrants whose economic system would eventually displace them. The process of colonization can be treated as a paradigm of nominalism of the colonizer and actualism of the colonized.

While the majority of deviation is one sided and easy to dismiss, centralization of power is tolerated though it leads to the other problems. Creation of duress can disperse the colonized while maintaining control over the settlers. The last 500 years or so of history have seen a steady increase in European nominalism into North America. Despite the American Revolution, which began at the Boston Tea party where revolutionaries dressed as natives rejected tea from the global economy, the global economy continues to encroach into North American society, as it has the entire world. Runaway debt and nominalism in North America now threatens to turn what, in 1492 was perhaps one of the worlds most actualistic countries, into one of the world's most nominalistic societies of the twenty first century. Where North America was once forced to accept the economic expansion of foreign countries, its uncontrolled obsession with its own economic expansion now encroaches on other lands.

Meanwhile, the United States Constitution, which can be considered a largely actualist document, is becoming increasingly viewed as annoying or inconvenient even by those who are sworn to uphold it and who ultimately gained their political power from it. The Declaration of Independence rejected European monarch as a political ideal and embraced the idea that "all men

David Billings

© Aketkov – Dreamstime.com

Figure 35 The castles of Europe are a nominalistic form of housing in that they are designed for conflict, require great debt, long time commitment and give nominal authority to its occupants. The "king" is often the one who lives in the "castle".

Introducing Economic Actualism

© Rinus Baak – Dreamstime.com

Figure 36 This abandoned Betatakin village from Arizona is an example of nominalistic housing from native America. While both nominalism and actualism existed in both Europe and North America in 1492, Europe was generally more nominalistic.

are created equal", an attempted rejection of centralized power. The Constitution set up a series of checks and balances to provide feedback and help prevent runaway power which could create inversions, though it did not use the word. The right to bear arms and the freedom of speech also add to this objective. In Canada, parliamentary procedures have contributed to these objectives as well. Throughout the world, monarchies have been eliminated or mitigated by new procedures.

©dhorsey – Dreamstime.com

Figure 37 Many governments in North America have been developing institutions and procedures to limit inversions, without using the word. Yet the processes of economic deviation still occur.

Yet in the present United States, pressure to reduce the effect of the Constitution has increased. Calls to register or confiscate handguns are louder with each mass shooting, many of which are involved with prescription medicines. One joint may have triggered mass murder in the film "Reefer Madness" and spawned an industry called the war on drugs, though very few if any murders have resulted from marijuana. Yet a continual rash of murders associated with prescription drugs yields only a massive nominalist silent form of authority.

Facing increasing voter discontent and a growing financial instability of the mainstream media, many call for restriction of free speech in the United States. The same pressures exist in

Canada. Orwellian phenomena have come to North America at an alarming pace.

© Idil Demir – Dreamstime.com

Figure 40 In his novel "1984" George Orwell described a totalitarian society that was enslaved by its own delusions. Much of our enforced Orwellian confusion comes from econo-addiction: our obsession with creating nominal wealth even at the expense of actual wealth but our unwillingness to change.

Other forms of deviation except centralization of power do not form a paradigm. They are simply wrong. Environmental damage and the other externalities are simply wrong. Idolatry is wrong, though it can be hard to identify. Uncertainty is bad. Duress is damaging. However, people make a lot of nominal money from these phenomena. The war on drugs in the United States funds one of the largest prison systems in human history. People make money from this. Failure to prevent health problems has created one of history's most dysfunctional health systems in the world, though many of us rely on it for our incomes even with good intent in our hearts. Duress over housing can increase economic participation, which people increase their nominal wealth with. So while these issues themselves are straightforward, they can create a society with a paradigm between nominal and actual economic wealth which is a source of confusion.

Nominalists often pair with actualists, though they don't use these terms to describe themselves. In marriage, one spouse can be the nominalist "bread winner" while the other can be the actualist "home maker". In cultural exchanges between nations, a nominalist charity can support an actualist's food consumption for a "dollar a day" while actualist countries can provide and escape from the "rat race".

Perhaps the greatest contributor of all to confusion however is an increased opinion of our own intelligence. Nominal authority: the ability to avoid any topic that might erode nominal wealth while increasing actual wealth, persuades all of us that we are smarter than we actually are. A recent poll by the web site YouGov determined that only 4% of Americans believe that they are less smart than the average citizen. Clearly this is an error. It stems largely from constant exposure to a culture of nominal intelligence. People assume that politicians, professionals, media and other authority figures achieve their position of authority by knowledge about actual wealth. But as we have seen, they are often given authority by their ability to increase nominal wealth instead.

Financial obligations often let nominal authority prevail over actual authority. In today's information age, everyone can gain access to information that makes authority figures seem to be in actual error. Yet it is the ability to avoid these facts and keep them from public consideration and discussion that often makes a modern authority figure. These nominal authorities keep a business cycle running which many of us are deeply committed to. Authority figures gain fame not just for actual knowledge, but also for the ability to maintain the business cycle and improve nominal wealth. When people fail to account for this, they can get an inflated sense of their ability which, by improving their perceptions of their own self-actualization on the Maslow hierarchy, can actually increase their economic confidence and participation in a vicious circle which further fuels the instability and growth of the business cycle.

The frustrating thing about nominal authority is not that nominalists are stupid. They can be extremely smart. The problem with them is that they weaponize what stupidity about actualism they do have with the utmost of their intelligence. It is not necessarily conscious. They merely seek with all of their willpower to concentrate on which side of their bread is nominally buttered. It makes them look stupid, even corrupt. But it is a choice of philosophy that comes from being deep inside of a business cycle so that it seems as if that is the only philosophy possible. Much of our psychology centres around this phenomenon. It is a dangerous, and addictive, form of ignorance which is described in "The Psychology of Economic Actualism" and also by describing the suicide of Judas in "Christianity as Economic Actualism".

Actualists object because they are often left to remedy situations nominalists will not acknowledge exist, even though they caused them and reaped nominal rewards from following these rules.

CULTURE

Given the above it is a wonder the human race has not blown up the Earth a dozen times already. Sevens billion hungry souls living on a worn out planet have to deal with inversions like environmental damage, loss of leisure, spiritual decay, error and damage due to a lack of prevention. We deal with loss of effectiveness through conflict, financial obligations and centralization of power. We deal with uncertainty not only from unavoidable duress but also from created duress and acquired duress. And for the most part, we must bear all of this desperation quietly. There are so many issues that we must give our consent to most of them through silence. Our efforts to both speak and listen are complicated by idolatry.

We live in an information age whose data and media creation, and consumption are without parallel in human history. The amount of information our society accumulates has been doubling at ever increasing rates. But when in conditions of duress such as conflict or lust for status, we may feel compelled to consume these sources of information, even when they seem annoying or bothersome.

© drx – Dreamstime.com

Figure 39 Many of us can feel stressed by modern media.

We now double our information in a little less than a year and the exponential effect of this over the last few centuries has resulted in billions of books, newspaper and magazine articles, scholarly publications, patents and letters. The arts of music and painting have been advanced with new methods of distribution as well. New forms of media have been created including motion pictures, video games and software. The internet as a means of distribution is exploding. Our time spent in education is longer than ever. Producing and consuming all of this culture is consuming an ever increasing amount of time, effort and expense.

Yet despite all of this culture, we are quieter in our desperation than ever. Our economy is dysfunctional and rife with the problems of both deviation and uncertainty. We are conflicted. Despite our nominal wealth, we are often not particularly happy. Our means of communication are not working properly.

To maintain our actual wealth while facing the constant creep of nominalism we must pay attention. Just as we have progressed up the Maslow pyramid from an obsession with eating calories to a consumption that creates health and self-actualization, we must change the way we consume communication. Four hundred years ago most people could barely read, if at all. The data available about their lives was a birth date, a date of death and a dash between the two on a tombstone. And most people throughout history have been buried in unmarked graves. Now, even our DNA is being placed on the record in some cases.

We can't consume media with the same reckless abandon our fact starved ancestors did and not expect to be injured by the process. Our modern society places a buffet of information in front of us. As we have seen, this is produced with both actual and nominal authority. Actual authority is media that makes us actually wealth. Nominal authority makes us nominally wealthy or, more likely, makes someone else nominally wealthy by maintaining a business cycle, or a society, that is dysfunctional.

Everyone has both actualist and nominalist tendencies. The switch to nominalism can often be unintentional or even subconscious. Many people do not even know what nominalism is. Yet they do it in their speech. They do can do it with their art or music. While commercial art, like advertising, may be more intentionally nominalist, the artist may still not be aware of the damage they are creating. Nominalism in art is often just accepted as the norm. It is seen as something to be accepted within the business cycle without question.

We have already discussed how some goods and services are more prone to become idols. Perceived long term rarity, distinctiveness and representativeness can combine to create an idol. When an idol raises the price of one product to unnatural levels, the other products within the defined set are lowered. This is what makes an idol and this can be expressed by the mathematical equation:

$$(9) \text{Id } v_0 V_0 + \text{Idv}_1 V_1 + \text{Idv}_2 V_2 + \ldots + \text{Idv}_N V_N = \text{Constant}$$

Idolatries are errors of perception and communication. Efforts to identify idolatries are complicated due to economic uncertainty. Measuring economic behaviour raises uncertainty as the economic participation for many products is often influenced by a few products which are consumed under duress, either unavoidable, created or acquired. Duress lessens people's ability to form rational opinions so while it is a separate phenomenon than idolatry, it can complicate efforts to weed out idolatry. Consent by silence also weakens economic feedback as it lessens people's ability to communicate and communication is central to feedback. But the style of communication can contribute to economic feedback as well.

Communication aids nominalism when it communicates using idols. Communication aids actualism when it communicates using icons. The terms "idol" and "icon" are typically used to describe communication of religious concepts, but these terms can be used when people communicate economically as well. An idol is an object that is worshipped.

Rather than being a piece of communication, it is an artifice which has value in and of itself.

When Moses was on Mount Sinai, his brother Aaron built a golden calf which the people worshipped as a deity. Idolatry was forbidden in the Ten Commandments which Moses had received on Mount Sinai so when he saw what the people were doing, he went into a rage. The theology which supported the golden calf is not mentioned in the Bible. Presumably, there was no theology, just a frustration and a rejection of the god of Moses.

People generally have a limited capacity for religion and spirituality. Often, Christmas and Easter are the only two church days of the year. While God presumably lives even outside of the walls of a church, many of us look to organized religion to form our first impressions of religion. The seeds of these first impressions of spirituality can grow into either noxious weeds or mighty oaks. But just as nominal wealth can be actual poverty, so too, can religious ritual can be spiritual decay. This was a major concern of Jesus as will be described in "Christianity as Economic Actualism: Ye Must Be Borne Again".

©Ziprashantzi- dreamstime.com

Figure 40 Lord Shiva statue at Murudeshwar in India is a 130 foot high idol of a Hindu deity which dominates attention in the area. Small trees are at the base.

© Ganesh4photolife – Dreamstime.com

Figure 41 A small scale idol factory in India is typical of religious idols made in many cultures.

Introducing Economic Actualism

© carrienelson1 – Dreamstime.com

Figure 42 Modern culture manufactures many cultural products which are part idol and part icon.

Replacing God with an idol during these scant hours of worship fits the mathematical expression of idolatry because the time spent worshipping a false idol will take time from worship of the true god, whatever that god may be. Worship of this fugitive true god would probably lead to further worship of it. Idolatry during those critical initial few hours takes away from legitimate spiritual journeys.

Rather than being an item of religious worship, an icon is an object or image used for religious communication. The purpose is to convey a concept, not impart a value. The word "icon" is not used in the King James Version of the Bible. The word "icon" was used in the early days of the Roman Catholic Church. But since those early days of the church, our use of communication has increased dramatically both in amount and variety.

The distinction between the two words, icon and idol, is important even when we are dealing with the economic usage of idols and icons, not just the theological usage. An icon is an image used to convey an intellectual or emotional message as quickly and effectively as possible. This message may not necessarily be truthful. Forces of nominal authority, criminal negligence or deceit and the tendency of the subject matter to form idolatries will help determine the truthfulness of a message. Truth is a major topic of philosophical study. But aside from the truthfulness of a message is its position on a continuum between icon and idol. Just as we are all on a continuum of being part actualist and part nominalist, so our modern communication is a continuum of being part idol, imparting value to an object, and part icon, conveying a message.

Where an idol could be expressed mathematically as:

(1) $Id\ v_0 V_0 + Idv_1 V_1 + Idv_2 V_2 + \ldots\ldots + Idv_N V_N = Constant$

An icon could be expressed mathematically as:

$Ic = K*(V_1 + V_2 + V_3 + \ldots\ldots V_n)$, where $K > 1$

Where Ic is the amount of resources, time and money, related to the item by both producer and consumer. K is a proportionality constant, a constant number. V1 to Vn are the values of all the goods and services effected by the communication. So what the formulaic expression for an icon is saying is that as you consume a message like a book, the value of your life which is effected by the book rises in proportion to how much you invest in the book. If you have diabetes and buy a book of recipes for diabetics, the increase in the value of your health and mood will be proportional to how much time you invest in the book.

But not all books have an iconic effect. I am a firm believer in the old leather bound encyclopaedias as a good reliable reference. Before they became obsolete by the internet, they had an iconic effect on my life as I referred to many of them constantly. When I tried to sell them in the dying days of their industry in the mid 1990's, I discovered that many people who used to buy encyclopaedias rarely used them, but were happy with their purchase because they "looked good on the shelf". If there was any message from the purchase, and encyclopaedias in those days were often a major investment, it was that "I respect academia" when people visited the home or office.

© vbaleha – Dreamstime.com

Figure 43 Many find profitable study from the study of iconic, religious trinkets such as this image of Madonna and Child. The difference between an idol and an icon is in their effects. An icon conveys meaning which yield practical benefits of some kind while an idol sells the value of the item, occupies the attention and diverts from other study. One man's icon can be another man's idol.

But the effect was primarily idolatrous. The books on the shelf imparted a value upon the office or owner. The encyclopaedias gave the image of scholarship, and the accompanying rise in value, without actually providing actual scholarship. This increase in the image of scholarship was probably accompanied by a decrease in the image of other offices or homes.

All communication is part iconic and partly idolatrous. A popular piece of music may express the feelings of youth in an iconic way. This will increase the feelings of collectivism amongst other youth and, sometimes, reach the heart of older generations as well. A piece of music can stand as a hallmark of an historical period, conveying to future generations what it felt like, and what we tried to feel like, during a certain time. A piece of music can join hearts at a dance, perhaps leading to a successful marriage. It can soothe the savage breast by pacifying the angry heart. Yet it can also arouse the depressed or melancholy. Concert experiences can help forge friendships. Musical jingles can have similar iconic impacts on business practices.

Yet music can also be idolatrous. Just as people have a limited capacity of religion, there is only so much music we can listen to and so much media we can consume. The popularity of one musician can either prevent or encourage the popularity of another musician. And some music gives more value to the performer than it creates value through a message.

Marshall McLuhan, a Canadian media theorist from the 1960's, was famous for his iconic message that "the medium is the message". Charles Dickens is widely recognized as one of history's greatest novelists. Yet in our time, we often criticize him for being wordy. His works were often published first as serials in newspapers. Newspapers were a relatively new medium and there was lots of paper to cover with ink and readers had time. So Dickens was paid by the word. While Dickens work had much to say about human nature and the English society he lived in, it also had subliminal messages that came from the medium itself. One of the messages of the newsprint fiction medium is that character's thoughts can be expressed by the words of a writer. When we read a novel we are buying the assumption that one person can verbally describe the thoughts and feelings of another, sometimes only by describing words and actions, in a way that a third party, the reader, can understand.

This medium also has a message about how long it takes to tell a story and how much time and effort the reader must invest. All genres have silent messages. Teenage comedies have different messages about language usage than high dramas. Westerns may not value language much at all but silently state that action is what is important. Cinema says that community grouping to view a film in a theatre adds to a theatrical experience. While television broadcasts say home comfort and potty breaks are good justifications for commercial breaks. Movies value capital investment and team efforts. Poetry values independent freedom of expression. Political speeches value practical social activation rather than simple amusement.

The usages of many words, considered vulgar, can carry a subliminal message that "I do not submit to the authority of the dictionary!". Using the word "ain't" repetitively in a political campaign is not done because it would appear subversive. Of course many vulgar words are worse than that.

A more sinister subliminal effect is in many of our communications however: the reduction of sales resistance. Freud believed that saying "no" to anything requires psychological energy and this energy is in finite supply. Not only modern media determined to tempt us to waste our limited time by giving us quests for useless knowledge, it also is determined to continually erode our sales resistance. The result is economic growth in areas where it often is not needed.

Many American grocery stores have magazine covers by the checkout of trim girls in bikinis etc. Nobody ever seems to object to these magazines but the pictures are strategically placed

© Tomnex – Dreamstime.com

Figure 44 Much of our popular culture revolves around creating flashy photographic images to reduce sales resistance, either in print, TV, internet or movies.

so it is very difficult in our society to buy food without looking at them. Most of these women, who are unnaturally beautiful in their natural state, are airbrushed for added enticement. The subliminal messages of this medium would seem to be that buying food makes you sexy. Buy more food. Reduction of sales resistance is common.

Yet much of our culture seems to revolve around reducing sales resistance. From the flashing lights and arousing music before our newscasts, to the anger inducing messages and to the annoying commercials, whose stated message is usually ineffective, each message has a psychological effect of weakening our resistance to the subliminal message that buying stuff will makes us happy. But audiences don't think much about these subliminal messages, although they consume considerable amounts of time, finances and mental efforts. They simply add to the idolatrous creation of value and lessen the iconic meaning.

And all messages are part icon, part idol. The Dow Jones Industrial Index is an icon if you are looking for a quick, convenient measure of investor confidence in overall corporate America. But it is an idol that exaggerates corporate importance on public news broadcasts every night if you are looking for an indicator of the economy's overall performance. Discretionary income or debt levels would be more iconic that that. A politician can be an icon for a political campaign but an overused idol after his term of office. A televised car commercial can be an icon regarding some special feature of the automobile but an idol as this commercial distracts from poor engine reliability.

Feedback is important for keeping economic deviation and uncertainty in check. We can only spend so much time communicating. Just as we smirk at Dickens for writing styles in response to being paid by the word, so future generations may look down at our media when, in a time of immense crisis, our media was aimed at monopolizing increasing amounts of viewer time and effort with trivia. Much of our communications does not contribute anything other than create an interest in seeing the sequel. Meanwhile, our lives and our society sinks deeper into econo-addiction.

© Scanrail – Dreamstime.com

Figure 45 Technology is transforming our ability to communicate and increasing our nominal communication exponentially. But this change in the nature of communication is altering our feedback mechanisms. The dysfunction of our society suggests that we are not adapting to this communication technology properly.

Chapter Five

Econo-Addiction

What we all want is actual wealth. We are all, at heart, actualists. But our modern lifestyle is a labyrinth. We start off as helpless babies in search of actual food and shelter. But we soon, very soon actually, must surrender to the centralized powers of our society. We start off with the light of our own souls to guide us, but we enter a darkened maze in search of another bright light to get our souls back to the beauty of our beginning. Unfortunately, many of us never see, and even stop looking for that second light. And even if we do see it, we are fortunate by that time to be able to pursue it. The maze has ways which force us to abandon pursuit of the light even when we do see it. Chasms block our path. The calls of sirens seduce us to abandon it. Our feet step on slippery slopes which drag us into pits. We are lucky, once we see the light again, to be in its pursuit, let alone guide other people to find it.

The maze which torments and confuses us is nominalism which, while we all realize is fundamentally just a tool to obtain actual wealth, often becomes a goal in and of itself. In "The Psychology of Economic Actualism" I describe how we all participate in both sides of the experiment of Pavlov's dog. Society requires us to both patiently wait for symbols and to create and use them. But many of us are unable to do both and we concentrate on one side or the other. For various reasons, our modern society often concentrates on creating and using symbols rather than on waiting for them.

This state of obsessing over nominal wealth, to the loss or neglect of actual wealth, is an econo-addiction. We have looked at the economic reasons for nominalism. Every business cycle has assumptions. These assumptions create nominal wealth with inevitable logical mechanisms that, without proper feedback, are inescapable. This nominal wealth is generated even when it damages actual wealth so long as the assumptions remain unchallenged. Inversions can make nominal wealth increase while actual wealth decreases such as from environmental damage, error, lack of leisure or spiritual malaise.

Effectiveness can be lost through conflict, financial obligation or centralization of power. Uncertainty exists since participation in a business cycle is often motivated by duress over a single good or service. This duress is sometimes created artificially or acquired. This duress affects all prices in an economy in uncertain ways due to irrationality. Often ineffectiveness can combine with inversion to create a bubble which motivates economic expansion through means of created duress.

Just as fuel, oxygen and a spark combine to create fire in a predictable manner, inversions combining with ineffectiveness and created duress combine to create an economic cancerous instability. Facing this complexity, we often consent with silence and our attempts to confront this confusion, and extinguish the economic fire, are complicated by forces of idolatry. These forces are all accepted when we are trapped within the business cycle. It all seems normal. It is when we step out of the nominalism of an economy that everything looks strange, even crazy. These are all economic forces.

But economies are affected by psychology as well, both on the individual level and the collective level. An addiction is defined as "dependence upon a habit". Living within a business cycle is the ultimate of habits. Business cycles that have uncontrolled growth can dominate every aspect of our lives: our time, our dreams, our money. We can even transfer the habit onto successive generations. Habits like alcohol or tobacco or any number of other addictions can leave us dependent upon them for short term happiness while they leave our long term habits in ruins. We have seen how business cycles can give us nominal rewards in the short term while leaving our long term actual wealth in ruins. Business cycles can be a bad habit and they can be a very difficult habit to break.

Addictions can have any number of psychological motivations. People drink alcohol to forget, to ease their loneliness, so they can relax, so they can be less inhibited, to be social. When they are mature they may drink because it allows them to be young again. When they are young, they drink because it allows them to be men. Other addictions also have a multitude of motivations. Econo-addiction can also have a variety of motivations.

The habits of a business cycle are so all encompassing, so varied and so overwhelming that we could likely find econo-addiction as a factor in every human problem. The love of money is the root of all evil. People participate in a business cycle because they are afraid, because they are loyal, because they are lazy, because they are overwhelmed, even if the duress that initially motivated them has been lessened. Virtually any human emotion or attribute has over the years persuaded people to continue to participate more in society. A business cycle is the life blood of its society.

And society itself is a centralization of power. But economics is not the only field with centralized power. Any social interaction centralizes power such as culture, language usage or religion. These all place some people in authoritative roles over others to some extent. Unlike other forms of inversion, centralization of power has a level that is "just right".

For without centralization of power, without society, mankind can not support itself. We are social animals. But one essential symptom of econo-addiction does exist. It is essential because it destroys feedback that is necessary to keep deviation and uncertainty in check.

The econo-addict glories in his shame. Nominalism is the everyday man's ticket to hubris,

© Inokos – Dreamstime.com

Figure 46 Most of us are conditioned to feel excitement when looking at an image of paper money. But when we enhance this excitement to the degree that we lose our ability to find actual happiness, we suffer econo-addiction.

contemptuous pride, and we are all nominalists to some extent. While we are all individuals, we are all also common in our own need for society. But when we embrace nominalism, we become more than animals, we become citizens. We become imbibed with the power and duties of the state. We wake with purpose and go to sleep with ambition. We realize this purpose is set out for us by other people and that our ambition has been crafted to mesh with the society. But with the constant messaging of our business cycle, these purposes and ambitions attain inevitability in our mind. They are unquestionable. People do things the way they are doing them because it has all been well thought out and planned. The business cycle even attains an image of divinity, as if it were pre-ordained.

As a result of this hubris, all manner of mistakes are excused, even encouraged. In many ways, the nominalist human can be seen as earth's lowest form of life. The nominalist human spends his valuable existence on creating worthless nominalist symbols to exchange for actual wealth, but often finds he no longer knows what actual wealth is. He freely joins a system of global destruction and possible annihilation just in hope of securing his essentials for life, but soon forgets what those essentials are, or in his pride anger and confusion, no longer cares. Yet, this state is encouraged because people can make money off it.

This encouragement comes not only when it hurts anonymous strangers but also when it hurts loved ones and even the person himself. We recognize that the creation of conflict and environmental damage is bad. But we also realize that war is good for the economy. War and the preparation for wars creates jobs and keeps people disciplined. Environmental damage is an inescapable by-product of commerce and progress.

Reducing leisure time is seen, not as a loss, but wholly as a source of wealth. No one pays you for leisure. Without nominalism of some kind, many of us do not know what to do with our leisure. Leisure is dangerous. It allows us to get into trouble. It particularly allows our kids to get into trouble.

They end up drunk on our front lawn, or worse, on somebody else's front lawn.

Econo-addiction is a shield which allows us to avoid such pratfalls. If we can just keep our nose to the grindstone of the current business cycle, the pesky problem of what to do with our spare time disappears. With nominalism, everything we do, every waking moment, can be recorded in a book somewhere as "good" and "proper". When we recognize that some of our nominalist efforts are actually less than divine, we have a ready-made excuse. We were "working".

After World War Two, when Nazi's were questioned about why they did such horrible things, their excuse was usually that they were "just following orders". Their actions were excused by the society of their time, so they just followed suit. Often in our society, people will justify an act because they are "just doing their job", as if being paid for an act automatically justifies it. And in a society of intense financial obligations such as ours, "just doing our job" is the justification for all kinds of acts.

Every litre of gasoline we burn creates about a cubic meter of exhaust. Just as our economic growth is now millions of time bigger than that of our ancestor's, so our consumption of energy, particularly fossil fuels, has grown exponentially. We see the danger to the climate: the wide scale destruction of the environment due to strip mining for coal, the global climate change, the sea level rise, deforestation and pollution. Yet we continue to burn vast amounts of fuel with moral impunity, even pride, because someone else has made a decision that this is how a business operates. A person making these decisions may not have actually existed. Or if they did, they were operating under a cancerous instability under which they felt they had no control.

Under the conditions of a certain business cycle, people are allowed, even encouraged to perform certain questionable acts in an unquestioning manner. It is as if the gods themselves have decreed that we follow a certain business cycle. To economist Adam Smith, an economy is led by an "invisible hand". The free market is a guide which, while not perfect, allows us to socialize: to fulfill our animalistic needs as individuals while organizing as a society.

Yet as we have seen, this "invisible hand" is often that of a pyromaniac sparking a match. We are in constant need of fire extinguishment. Yet due to idolatrous reasons and uncertainty, we usually watch passively or even blindly as the fires, even those created by our own actions, destroy our world, our society, our towns, our families and even ourselves.

The fire is nominalism. Just as alcohol can entice us to destroy our lives, nominalism can entice us into a life of destruction. But we are not ashamed. We see glory in it. To habitually find glory in the shame of adhering to a business cycle is the most pervasive addiction in modern North American society.

This pride is a symptom of econo-addiction. When a person gets drunk on alcohol and suffers in the manner of vomiting or passing out, he feels shame. He gets warnings when he sees other drunks. He provides his own feedback. When a smoker starts to hack, he senses his own folly and thinks of all the premature deaths.

But when an econo-addict starts to go astray, this feedback is usually lacking. He feels no shame. Two reasons exist for this lack of feedback. First he often views his suffering as a source of pride. The econo-addict suffers the excesses of his own efforts in the name of the greatest show on earth: the prominent business cycle of his time. For marketing reasons, everyone in an economy plays a unique role that they alone, out of seven billion people, have been deemed most worthy to perform.

Every newspaper boy has, out of the entire world's population, been judged best able to do his position, even if his accession to this throne is based mainly on the proximity of his residence and his ability to work for a lower wage with an acceptable service. The newspaper boy may not even read very well and so is in a poor position to judge the worthiness of the product he delivers. But when he completes his route, he feels a sense of pride in his accomplishment. The writing may have been slanted, or may have been poorly expressed, but that was not his job. He completed his task within the business cycle. He feels no sense of guilt for the trees which were killed for him to accomplish his task. No reason to regret any lies that were in the paper. The more tired his legs at the end of the route, the greater his pride, for he did it in the name of the greatest show on earth, even if his part in it was rather minor and subservient.

The paper boys' suffering for the nominalist cause may be minor, but the trend continues in adults whose role is more authoritative. Unlike many of us, the paper boy probably shows a profit for his work. His sacrifice is minor. But the characters described in his newspaper and the patrons who read it may not be as prosperous. They too have acquired a role in the greatest show on earth.

Other forms of addiction often play primarily with the lower pleasure centers of the brain such as feelings of animalistic pleasure. But econo-addiction plays with pleasure from men's need to contribute to society. The people in the newspaper may engage in conflicts or deviations, or promote idolatries or uncertainty, but it is in the service of the business cycle. The drunk's suffering is viewed as an anti-social or perverted social act. The econo-addict's act is for the pursuit of a greater cause. Due to idolatry, ineffectiveness and the lack of leisure, the business cycle maintains its assumptions because it can not afford to take the time to change these assumptions.

Changing assumptions requires a critical activity: negotiation. The word "negotiation" comes from the Latin roots meaning "not leisure" Negotiation requires effort. It requires feedback which requires constant vigilance. Negotiation is a burden that robs us of the leisure time we have. Without leisure time, time free from econo-addiction, we can not change the assumptions of the business cycle. Surrendering to the business cycle is a form of laziness, but under the nominalist assumptions of the business cycle, it is "work". This assumption is not open to debate.

Under these assumptions, suffering is not due to laziness or a mistake in negotiation, but a sacrifice for the higher cause. Misery becomes a sign of wisdom, not a foolish inability to find joy in life. Many a nominalist views a person who shows happiness as clownish. "Certainly anyone who smiles must either be stupid or, even worse, not in tune with the business cycle." To the econo-addict, happy people are idiots and untrustworthy. It is an example of how spirituality becomes an inversion. The unhappier you are, the more dour and serious your countenance, the wiser and more worldly you must be and the more money you must be worth.

Jesus spoke of this in his days. He criticized the Hebrew priests for wearing long faces when they fasted to announce their suffering to the world. Jesus often talked about people as being like cups who were clean on the outside, in the face they showed to the world, but dirty on the inside where it really mattered and where God had to look on them. These were people who lived from religious tithing. Yet they presented their work as a great sacrifice in the name of their community. These dirty cups can be understood as the nominalist within all of us.

In actuality, charity is a gift given in a spirit of collectivism. An actualist, and we are all actualists in our best moments, gives cheerfully because he is happy that he has resources to spare and knows the assumptions of the business cycle have given to him while it has been less generous with others. And every economic transaction has an aspect of charity to it. An economic transaction is a collectivist act. The traditions of the times, the abandonment of negotiation in the name of expeditiousness, have bound both parties into a social act.

When they are actualists, both parties are cheerful to be able to agree socially on a transaction.

Yet to nominalists, and we are nominalists to some extent, charity itself is a bit of a contest. The one who displays the most misery, the most unhappiness with the social situation, is the one who pushes future negotiation most into his own favour. This sounds ugly but it is a common form of econo-addiction. Support of the business cycle is a holy act in their eyes which justifies all suffering and, unlike alcoholism, the more suffering in the name of the business cycle the more charity you deserve. The nominalist tends to think he has earned his charity, making it more of a demand than a request.

Competition for low status is an inescapable economic activity. We all sell ourselves in this manner as a process of negotiation or we will not be in business long, left to wholly earthly means. Suffering in the name of the business cycle is nominally recorded and this nominalism is necessary for negotiation when it occurs, even if the nominal records are partially erroneous. Nominalism shields us from the overwhelming grind of negotiation.

Negotiation is difficult, particularly for some of us. It requires information. It requires us to compete for low status but it also requires us to build trust with each other and display honour. Once the business cycle is set in play, all of this is done for us. Only heaven can seem to intervene for the man who dares to do business but will not compete for charity.

But the relationship between a free spirited actualist and a nominalist, whose beliefs are hooked into the business cycle, are one sided. The nominalist has the status quo on his side. Whether it being the going union rate, the building code, the common business practice, the letter of the law, the dictation of spelling in the dictionary or the local customs, much of what we do and how we behave are really not up for negotiation until some sort of radical social change occurs due to pent up frustration.

When a nominalist corrects an actualist, and there is often a need for correction, it is called "education". When an actualist corrects a nominalist, and there is often a need for correction, it is called "bad manners", "insubordination", "rebellion" or "treason". Many words with negative connotations exist. These attitudes help expand the set of activities under the current business cycle by reducing feedback but as we have seen, feedback is essential to prevent an economy from econo-addiction.

Yet all societies struggle with this issue of conformity versus deviance, which is not to be confused with deviation. Deviance is turning from the norms of a society. Economic deviation is creating wealth nominally while creating actual poverty and ineffectiveness. But every business cycle, and every special interest within that business cycle, struggles with this issue. A young adult may struggle to accept the standards of dress and behaviour within the school system. But as he rejects it and adopts the conventions of a local street gang, he finds that their conventions of dress and behaviour though different, are just as stringently enforced. Usually, many of these conventions we are asked to adopt are termed a privilege, not a source of suffering.

For surrendering to the nominalist assumptions is a ticket into the greatest show on earth. Nominalism not only skews our perception of suffering, it also skews our perceptions of guilt and self-worth. Many a toady on the school playground teams up with the local bully to torment the local younger children. Associating with the bully allows the toady to exercise the uncharitable aspects of his character without being totally responsible himself. He is after all, just following orders. He could not carry out his work of tormenting smaller children without the endorsement of the bully. He needs a collective to belong to, or else he would be forced to verbally defend his actions solely by himself. This would be a very lonely task. But belonging to the bully, or a small clique of similarly minded people, satisfies both his need for individually expressing his superiority over others and for belonging to a group.

Adhering to the nominalist cause can create a similar lack of guilt later in life while it skews our perception. Joining the financial elite can allow you not only great financial wealth compared to your inferiors, but it allows you a "trickle down" philosophy where the poor will benefit from the benevolent aspects of your school yard tyranny. Just as the toady submits to the bully to join the greatest team on the school yard, we adults submit, usually under duress, to join the business cycle.

Inevitably, this centralization of power enhances the wealth of some individuals more than others. It may even victimize some. But unlike other aspects of economic deviation, centralization of power is a necessary evil for human existence. We need an amount of centralization which is "just right", an amount that allows us to be both individuals and part of a community. But this leads to dissonance between social groups, the driving force behind politics as will be described in "The Politics of Economic Actualism".

Econo-addiction, unlike other addictions, traps us into behaviours which can be very anti-social but which we feel little remorse for because they are done in the name of social authorities which we select but have very little control over. Joining the nominalist set of assumptions is not only expedient, it is also self-aggrandizing. If we lack the time, information or skills at negotiating, and we all do, we can join a union or trade association and have our wage negotiated for us. If we lack the skills or credibility to build a home that can be resold in a global marketplace in twenty years, and we all do, we can adhere to a building code. If we lack the wisdom to live peaceably with others at the subjects of our own whimsy, and we all do, we can adhere to the law. Likewise we can adhere to business customs to interact with strangers due to our lack of charm. Also we can adhere to the dictates of the prevalent grammar and spelling if our ability to communicate without them is insufficient. Adhering to the dictates of nominalism defends us from all manner of our own inabilities. It often doesn't matter if the figurehead we follow is lawless.

Yet nominalism can also rob us of our creativity and persuade us into destructive behaviours. As we have seen, even without individual malice, economic forces can make conformity to a society an anti-social act. Without constructive feedback, the assumptions of a business cycle can be more than just erroneous, they can be calamitous. But nominalism removes from us the guilt and shame that other forms of addiction provide. When we adhere to a business cycle, we can always say that someone else is to blame for our actions.

Often we do not blame those in authority for the destruction that occurs when we follow their orders. We blame actualists, those living on the periphery of society who are trying to create actual wealth. A business cycle trapped by a combination of inversion, ineffectiveness and duress is like a fire ignited by fuel, oxygen and a spark. It grows. To those inside the initial site of combustion, this can be a cause of great suffering. Their actual wealth declines while their nominal wealth increases. Their spirituality suffers yet they are unable to explain this suffering without rebelling against the business cycle which they have adopted. This inversion can only be remedied on their own personal level by expanding the fire to other peoples or geographies or by increasing the participation of those already involved. The early adopters have their personal actual wealth increased by taking a percentage of the nominal wealth created by this expansion.

They then "flip" this nominal wealth for the actual wealth they crave. It is like a pyramid scheme which must have an ever growing number of new entries to provide wealth for those initiators at the top. Unlike pyramid schemes however, the business cycle is imbibed with the moral authority of the business cycle. Those who resist joining the business cycle must be either "evil" or "lazy" not to see its valour. Attempts to alter the business cycle to fit the perceptions of newcomers are often viewed with similar sentiment.

Nominalists are hindered from seeing their own addiction since they are often not the ones personally injured by many of the damages. The damages are distributed by the centralized power to other people. In an expanding global economy these victims may be far removed from the causation of error. Yet the nominalist only sees the victims' misfortune, not their innocence. The poverty of others, even when it comes from the business cycle the nominalist believes in, further persuades the nominalist to believe in the business cycle since those on the periphery of it are in need of so much charity.

But people join nominalist belief systems with the goal of creating actual wealth, even if it is only their own personal actual wealth. We may not be able to express it, but we often have a funny subconscious feeling that the business cycle is not perfect, that it could use correction. Yet some of the rot within a nominalist system can very hard to acknowledge, especially when you have dedicated yourself to its expansion and have lost your effectiveness to reduce your participation.

Nominalism eats babies! It is an infant chomping monster, a mindless mechanistic juggernaut enslaved into an obsessive abuse of future generations, either at home or abroad. That may be a blunt way to say it, but it needs to be said. The only way people trapped in an inversion can generate more actual wealth for themselves is to expand the system and take a percentage of the nominal wealth created and then convert it into actual wealth for themselves. This requires us to expand the business cycle to children and foreigners.

In nominalist eyes, this consumption of novices may even seem benevolent. Not willing to consciously admit the nominalist system is unsustainable, the nominalist will gladly educate the next generation on "how the world works" and the "way of the future". In the process the next generation becomes even more hopelessly saddled with student loans, mortgages and government debt.

Nominalism also often derides the requests for change from new inductees as immature or unseasoned. Children see a vast opportunity in the world around them but are not in tune with the "harsh economic reality". While environmental damage has, and will continue to create much hardship, a lot of this harsh economic reality is due to the errors of the current and previous business cycles.

© Paulus Rusyanto – Dreamstime.com

Figure 47 According to USA Today, in 2011 student loans in the United States totalled more than $1 trillion and exceeded total credit card debt.

We have seen how inversions, ineffectiveness and duress can combine to create cancerous economic instabilities. Yet the nominalist, and we are all nominalists, has difficulty in seeing this process. While he hopes to cash in his nominalist chips for actual wealth, for the moment he is committed to the problem at hand, increasing nominal wealth. Actual wealth can seem like a strange dream he had long ago and to which he'll never return. Buddha once said that happiness is a journey and not a destination. But the nominalist forgets that saying. He sets actual wealth as a destination and as a result, he never reaches it. The destination of actual wealth can become a fable to him. In the process, he prevents the rest of the world which is within his influence from reaching it as well.

Nominalists are the worst bigots! With nominalism the way the world works is not open for negotiation since there is no time available. He is too busy chasing nominal wealth. Everything has been pre-judged and that prejudice is without correctable error. Conflict is a good thing. We can profit from environmental loss. Error drives more sales. People who can not accept these truths are slothful trouble makers and it is the nominalists job, in fact his sad and solemn duty, to make these people see the error of their ways and join the business cycle.

For the business cycle is in desperate need of growth and, since the business cycle is the greatest show on earth, the world is also in need of growth of the business cycle. Despite its intrinsic errors, the business cycle can be very dogmatic and judgmental. It views itself as the way the world runs, when it is often best described as the way the world fails. And when the world does fail, to the nominalist it is probably because not enough people followed orders, not because they withheld feedback.

But despite the bravado in our nominalism, we also harbour great doubts about the way the world commonly operates. We may rarely discuss it but we see it. And we can not help but feel that our actual position is declining. Surely the weight of our sacrifices for nominalism have paid off for someone. Our actual poverty from our nominal efforts must be the result of exploitation.

Someone else in the society is taking advantage of us. We nurture these pet peeves: the government bureaucrat with his fat pension, the rich capitalist with his off shore bank account, the unionized workers with their benefits and easy work conditions, the welfare recipients with their leisure time. The list goes on. While many of us suffer from the defects of a nominalist society more than others, this vilification of other classes can have serious psychological ramifications. As nominalists, we have dedicated our lives to society's greatest show on earth. We may have our faults but at least we are not "those people".

So nominalism can not only give us our self-image, it can give us an image of what we are not: the people who we vilify. The frustration of living a nominalist existence gives our human nature a need to identify the people who messed us up, along with the rest of society. The labourer can vilify the boss. The boss can vilify the indolent worker. The worker can vilify the disabled. The disabled can vilify the investor. We can all find someone to vilify. And almost everyone can agree in unison to vilify the politician or the central planner. Surely, if we were those people in their circumstances, we would perform better and society would gain actual wealth, instead of nominal wealth.

We look for and find human culprits for our common dilemma, when the problem is often due to philosophic error in the economic system. We all think we are creating someone else's actual wealth from our actual suffering. Instead, everyone is really creating nominal wealth for others.

Eventually, the actual situation catches up with us. When it happens to us as an individual, we are faced with a situation where the nominal reality is exposed as a fairy tale which has deluded us and consumed our lives. We have spent our whole life chasing our own tail in a nominalist labyrinth and have nothing of actuality to show for it. Just as a drunk may hit rock bottom when he falls asleep while driving or loses his job, an econo-addict may hit rock bottom with a stress attack or financial crisis. He may have alcoholism as a symptom too.

But while the alcoholic will see himself as the problem when he realizes his addiction to drink, the econo-addict has less of himself to point his finger at. The econo-addict obeyed all the rules. He did everything he was supposed to do. He followed the system and it led him into an actual abyss, with not so much as a recognition or thank you from the people who exploited him for what he believes was their actual gain.

© Ashestosky – Dreamstime.com

Figure 48 When an alcoholic struggles to see the dysfunctions in his life he is likely to recognize that alcohol could be a problem. But many people fail to see that nominalism could be misleading their life. Alcoholics and other addicts who fail to see a danger from their habit are usually seen to be at particular risk.

He may have an "actualist epiphany", where he realizes almost in a religious experience that "nominalism is pointless", though he does not use such colorless words. To many of us, econo-addiction is a free floating anxiety. We know something is wrong but feel powerless to correct it and feel it would be pointless to identify it. But on an individual level, a crisis may suddenly exist where we feel something must change.

When an alcoholic reaches his bottom, he may join a group like Alcoholics Anonymous. There he will learn he must admit his addiction and then surrender to a higher power. Only a higher power can pick him up from his addiction. When an econo-addict can no longer sustain his place in the business cycle, he too will turn to a higher power. Though when his addiction is so poorly defined he may be like one of Konrad Lorenz's ducklings. Lorenz was a psychologist who hatched some duck eggs from scratch. The ducklings "imprinted" upon Lorenz, thinking that because he was the first face they saw, that he was their mother. Lorenz believed the ducklings were genetically programmed to imprint on the first face they saw.

An econo-addict after an epiphany may also imprint, though often on an ideological cause or leader who helps him regain a spot in the pulsating flock of humanity. An actualist epiphany can occur at any age. Many a teenager will glumly pronounce that "school sucks" one day or many a disgruntled business may will say the "system stinks". Housewives may find difficulty finding purpose. Voters may throw their hands up in dismay. The alienation of the individual in our society from the business cycle is constant. While it is usually not well expressed, this alienation can often be seen as a free floating anxiety about nominalism.

Yet those addicted to nominalism often feel no shame since they are following "the rules". The source of authority for these rules is often unimportant to them and can easily come from the unspoken habits of the business cycle. In Jeremiah 5:31 it is said that the priests ruled by their own authority and the people liked it that way. It is more than an attitude of "everyone else is doing it". The attitude is usually "this is the way that it is done". It takes imagination to consider possibilities outside of the society you live in. Many nominalists lack this needed imagination, even when the life they lead seems to desperately need a change.

But more so than actualists, nominalists tend to look for authority figures from their society such as individuals or trends for direction rather than their own initiative, particularly during transitions. When they look for a higher power to submit to, their accumulated duress may not allow them to choose rationally. Factions can form from the shared irrationalities of social cliques or special interest groups. These groups are often antagonistic to each other as the labyrinth of nominalism creates all manner of imaginary pet peeves to blame for the mess. While many special interests blame each other, they can be intimately dependent upon each other as they suffer from various incarnations of the same unspoken curse, econo-addiction.

A TALE OF TWO VIEWPOINTS: NOMINALISM AND ACTUALISM

Nominalism is an inescapable and problematic aspect of life. What actually happens is always altered by the act of measuring it nominally. This is true regardless of the time period or the culture, though some cultures have more of a problem with nominalism than others. Nominalism and actualism are always eyeing each other, criticizing each other, even if they do not have a verbal framework for use in description.

Nominalist and actualist tendencies even exist within the same person. We start off by defining actual goals. Then we devise methods to accomplish them socially by getting nominal recognition with plans to redeem this later for actual rewards. Even if the actual reward we seek is recognition itself, we often have to obtain nominal accomplishments we do not want before getting nominal rewards we actually want.

But actualists and nominalists do not get along. They constantly quarrel, not understanding each other but forced to work with each other by a system that demands their participation without explaining how or why. Of course, nobody goes through life with a name tag on their label of "actualist" or "nominalist" because we all are in essence actualists. We want actual happiness and actual wealth. But the process of society and its centralized power requires us to be nominally measured. So we are also, part nominalist.

To the actualist within us, the nominalist is a pest who views every act we do as an excuse to tax us and regulate us purely for their own benefit. An actualist does not see a need for society to help with anything. Society is a juggernaut that crushes anything of actual value in its path because it views anything of actual value as competition to its twisted and perverted, nominalist, view of life. An actualist could get by with very little help from society, except for the fact that society has so many other people that misbehave who must be kept under control, both for their own good and for the good of everyone else. Nominalists really don't contribute anything. They're overhead that must be minimized as much as possible since they refuse to do any meaningful work.

Their labour of choice is simply to criticize others. But they rely on others to do actual work on their behalf. They are constantly asking actualists to bail them out with actual contributions to solve their nominal debts and neurotic compulsions. They don't live in the real world, but in an artificial world of their own creation that has unattainable and unnecessary demands. But they won't listen to reason. Rather than put in an honest day's work they demand that others work for them and then expect to be bailed out by some actual Santa Claus or something, a figure who does not exist and if he did would want nothing to do with them.

To the actualist, nominalists have no respect for anything of value but view everything with a reckless attitude of "let's tax it to death". They are constantly devising some twisted social initiative but there is nothing new under the sun that some government has not already tried. So why bother. The world would be a much better place if the nominalists only interacted with each other in their own community and thus withered away from the face of the Earth.

To the nominalist within us, and we are all nominalists to some extent, the actualist is a lawless nuisance who uses every excuse to ignore social convention and the rule of law for their own selfish benefit. When caught within the nominalist labyrinth, we do not see a need for actualism in anything. The nominalist business cycle creates ever increasing happiness and wealth.

Talk of actual happiness outside of the business cycle is just an excuse not to pitch in and help the social effort. There is something twisted and wrong about an actualist. They seek to "mitigate the damages" done by society but do not realize that without the current business cycle, nothing would exist. We would be wretched, starving, naked miserable rats trying to dig roots up from the frozen ground without society. Actualists don't really contribute anything. Actualists are nay sayers whose efforts must be minimized as they refuse to do any meaningful work. Their labour of choice is to criticize others. But they rely on nominalists to do the practical work on their behalf. They are constantly asking nominalists to bail them out because they follow silly pipe dreams and neurotic compulsions. They don't live in the real world but in an imaginary world of their own impossible and unattainable demands. But they refuse to listen. Rather than obey the rules and put in an honest day's work, they demand that society work for them and then bail them out like Santa Claus or something, a figure who does not exist and if he did, would put them on the naughty list and have nothing to do with them.

To the nominalist, actualists respect nothing of value but have a reckless attitude of "let's do it our own way", which contributes nothing but creating a lot of unnecessary headaches and work. There is nothing new under the sun and if it was worth doing something differently we would know about it. The world would be a much better place if the actualists only interacted with each other so that only they would have to endure their own lawlessness and thus wither away from the sight of the Earth.

The above dialogue is fictional but the nominalist and actualist ideals often do not appreciate or understand each other, even when arguing within the same company. The actualist versus nominalist argument festers because it is not verbalized. Like many forms of measurement, the process of economic measurement is a source of uncertainty. When we attempt to measure rational behaviour with money, we risk altering the definition of rationality due to the assumptions of that business cycle. Often, our economic measurement tells us we are creating wealth when in fact, wealth is being lessened. Many forms of inversions create this illusion. When an inversion is coupled with a loss of effectiveness under duress, we often feel that we have no choice but to expand our nominal economy in an attempt to create a larger nominal pie of which we can take a sliver and convert into actual wealth.

Attempts to modify this situation with feedback are often complicated by idolatrous communications. People don't, or can't, listen. Caught in a trap of addiction to economic growth, many economies grow through created and acquired duress. While this seems like a collection of truisms, we often fail to analyze what is happening and the economy becomes a dark and seemingly endless maze of traps and snares which rolls upon ocean waves of mass desire. It is easy to fall victim to nominalism. But like many poisons, we simply lose consciousness. Our perception dims from its effects and we perish.

Afterword

Nominalism is a threat to us all, yet we depend on it. As human beings, we rely on society throughout our lives. Without the herd, we quickly perish and without nominal records of some type, even if they are only unspoken traditions, the herd can not exist.

So our existence is a constant balancing act. We are dependent from birth on some degree of centralization of power. Yet that dependence is an inversion in that it creates nominal wealth while it can decrease actual wealth. This is a gateway for econo-addiction into our lives. Dependence on centralization leads to other inversions and ineffectiveness. Yet duress prohibits us from leaving the society and even increases our participation, often to artificial levels.

But applying economic actualism, the study of how the nominal and actual economic reality get confused, can help us to manage the problem. Just as it would be a mistake to neglect our health because we are certain to die, it is a mistake to neglect to manage nominalism because we are fated to suffer its effects.

The numbers of economic growth suggest that we each consume 20 million times the nominal wealth of our ancestors. Yet our actual growth is less. We have a chance to improve. The kingdom of God is within us, the actual reality, not our nominal records.

Economic actualism is a new branch of the social sciences which is sure to have many applications in numerous fields at a time when it is sorely needed, though it has always been needed. In good times, in bad times, and in crisis, managing nominalism yields opportunity for life.

Index

Abortion	72	Clothing	113, 118
Abundance, Perception of	55	Cognitive Dissonance	144, 145
Actualism, blame on	183	Cold War	134
Actualism, journey of	132	Collective vs Collectivism	143
Addictions	122	Collectivism	138
Alternate means of production	30	Colonialism	53
		Colonialism as Nominalism	150
Anarchism, Left-Right	136	Colonial-Native Paradigm	149
Anomie	105, 130	Communication	52, 54, 121
Assumptions	10	Communication as Icon and Idol	160, 163
Assumptions of Business cycle	149	Communists	133
Auschwitz	52	Complexity	62, 130
Authorities	125	Conflict	24, 33
Authority, actual	126	Conflict as idol	94
Authority, Nominal	126, 147	Conflict as ineffectiveness	92, 94
Bargains, unnatural	53	Conflict, Numerous Effects	92
Basic Needs	59	Conflict, Various Forms	92
Branding	22, 32, 50	Confusion	3, 25, 38, 133
Bubble, economic	89, 96	Consent	8
Business Cycle	110	Consent by Silence	123
Business Cycle as a Set of Habits	172, 175	Constitution	151
Celebrities	51	Credibility	125
Centralization and feedback	96	Culture	157
Centralization as ineffectiveness	95	Currency Acceptance	146
		Currency as Deviation	146
Centralization, need for	95	Currency as idol	51
Charity	179	Currency Changes	10
Charity as a Contest	179	Currency, perfect	8
Class Conflict	141	Currency, Validity of	147
		Defence	121

Deforestation	69
Dependence on Centralization	25
Dependence on Centralization and Feedback	34
Derivatives	11
Deviance	181
Deviation	3, 16, 43
Deviation and Feedback	28
Deviation, Justification of	155
Deviations	108
Dictatorship	106
Discourse	132
Discretionary Income	90
Distinctiveness	49
Distinctiveness, Perceived	53
Diversity	148
Division by Zero	29
Division of Labor	130
Duress	103, 107, 11, 114
Duress, Created	115
Econo-addiction	4, 5, 35, 39, 171
Econo-addiction, imprinting	189
Econo-addiction, lack of shame	174, 178
Econo-addiction, Motivations	173
Economic Actualism	1
Economic Growth	36
Economic Growth, as a Fire	108
Economic Growth, Unstable	108
Economic Measurement	1
Economic Participation	116
Economic Theory, early	69
Employment Issues	102
Environmental Damage as Inversion	76
Envy	33, 81
Epiphany, Actualist	188
Error	21
Error and Prevention of Damage	34
Error as Inversion	87
Escapism	122
Esteem	60
Expertise	125
Externalities	16
Externalities and Feedback	29, 30
Federal reserve, US	91
Feedback	169
Financial Obligations	23, 32, 89
First Principle	7
Fishing as Economic Growth	36
Fishing Industry	17
Flocks of Birds	100
Food	109, 111
Fractional Reserve Banking	91
Free Floating Anxiety and Nominalism	131, 188
Free market	49
Fuel	69, 112
Full and Fair Consideration	101
Globalism	38, 63
Gluttony	82
Gold	9, 48
Governance	27
Greed	79
Growth	4
Health and Inversion	72
Healthcare industry	70
Housing	113
Icon, Mathematical Expression for	164
Icons	163
Idolatries	22
Idolatries and Feedback	32
Idolatry	43, 160
Idolatry, Identifying	164
Idolatry, Mathematical Expression of	65
Idolatry, Three Elements	47
Idols	48

Idols, no central regulation	49	Media	63
Ind Expresssion vs Exp of Ind	143	Medical Statistics, Inversion of	72
Individualism	138	Meditation	86
Ineffectiveness	23, 88	Misery Presented as Wisdom	179
Ineffectiveness and Feedback	32	Misrepresentation	64
Inefficiencies	22	Moses	161
Infant Mortality and Abortion Inversion	73	Natural Resources	69
		Negligence	126
Infant Mortality, Historical	71	Negotiation	178
Information Age	156, 158	New Orleans	47
Information, Consumption of	158	Noah	36
Instability	14	Nominal Mask, Juxtaposition of	133
Intelligence of Nominalism	157		
Intelligence, Self Opinion	156	Nominalism	132
Introspection, Loss of	64	Nominalism and Bigotry	186
Inversion, Mathematical Expression of	67	Nominalism as Antisocial	183
		Nominalism as Bullying	181
Invisible Hand	177	Nominalism, Abuse of Underlings	184
Irrationality	114		
Laissez Faire Economics	104	Nominalism, Blindness of	185
Language	100, 145	Nominalism, Causes of	171
Left Right Paradigm	133	Nominalism, Journey of	171
Leisure	18, 84	Nominalist Causes	175
Leisure and Feedback	31	Nominalist, Journey of	171
Life Expectancy and Abortion Inversion	73	Nominalists	85
		Nominalists, removed from damages	184
Life Expectancy at Birth, Historical	70		
		North American History	111
Life Expectancy at Conception	73	North American Natives as Actualists	150
Locales	51		
Love and Belonging	60	North American, Created Duress	116
Love of Money	5, 7, 39		
Lunar Fishery	37	North American, Housing and food	118
Lust	81		
Marriage Cycle	129	Obligation and Econo-Addiction	172
Marx, Karl	33, 134, 140, 142		
Maslow's Pyramid	58, 59	Opportunity from Actualism	40
Maslow's Pyramid and feedback	61	Orwell, George	98, 155
		Paradigm, Collectivistic-Individualistic	136, 137
McLuhan, Marshall	166		

Paradigm, Left-Right	133	Soccer, children's	135
Participation	27	Speciousness	148
Partnership, Actualist and Nominalist	156	Spice Trade	45
		Spirituality	18, 78
Pharmaceuticals	74	Spirituality and Feedback	31
Politics, Western	134	Spock	99
Potato	115	Status	121
Prevention of Damage	20	Sublimation	15
Prevention of Loss	88	Supply and Demand Curve	26
Price	4	Technology	62
Pride	80	Theory	1
Principles, Three	3	Third Principle	25
Protest	14	Thoreau, Henry David	10, 108
Purgatory	9	Tulip Craze	44
Quantity	4	Uncertainty	3, 7
Quarrelling, actualists versus nominalists	191	Unworthiness	55
		Value, Intrinsic without Currency	148
Quiet desperation	108	Video tape formats	90
Rational Behaviour	103	Virtues, Seven Heavenly	82
Rationality	7	Vulgarity	167
Relationships	125	Walden Pond	108
Relationships, Actualist with Nominalist	180	Woodstock	52
		Words as Idols	52
Religion	122	Wrath	79, 190
Ritualism-Spirituality paradigm	161	Youth and Conflict	120
		Zero Sum Gain Idolatry	56
Robber-Barons	133		
Sales resistance	82		
Sales Resistance, reduction of	167		
Scarcity	49		
Scarcity, Perceived	58		
Second Principle	16		
Security	60		
Self Image of Right and Left	140, 141		
Self-actualization	61		
Services as idols	50		
Silence	9, 109		
Sins, Seven Deadly	78		
Sloth	80		

About the Author

Like most of us, David Billings has spent a life time watching society fluctuate between actualist and nominalist perspectives with both curiosity and dismay. David's quest began on a camping trip in Northern Ontario when he was eight years old and caught a fish with his bare hands during an eclipse of the sun. The long drive home, with its progressive re-entry into society gave him a sense of mission: to find out why we go to such lengths to escape a society which we go to such lengths to create and sustain. The wordless wonder of an eight year old was carried through university degrees in commerce, social organization and human relations as well as economics from Western University plus biological engineering from the University of Guelph. He briefly taught in the business department of Sheridan College. Without accepting any major corporate responsibilities, he has been given a long lasting critical perspective by working as an independent handyman.

www.ingramcontent.com/pod-product-compliance
Lightning Source LLC
Chambersburg PA
CBHW030931180526

45163CB00002B/529